HAL LEONARD KEYBOARD STYLE SERIES

BEGINNING ROCK KEYBOARD

THE COMPLETE GUIDE WITH AUDIO!

PLAYBACK+
Speed • Pitch • Balance • Loop

To access audio visit:
www.halleonard.com/mylibrary

Enter Code
"3154-0132-8646-0331"

BY MARK HARRISON

ISBN 978-1-4234-8513-1

T0057690

HAL•LEONARD®
7777 W. BLUEMOUND RD. P.O. BOX 13819 MILWAUKEE, WI 53213

In Australia contact:
Hal Leonard Australia Pty. Ltd.
4 Lentara Court
Cheltenham, Victoria, 3192 Australia
Email: ausadmin@halleonard.com.au

Visit Hal Leonard Online at
www.halleonard.com

INTRODUCTION

Welcome to *Beginning Rock Keyboard*. If you're looking for a beginner-friendly introduction to playing rock keyboard, then you've come to the right place! This book takes you from the very basic concepts to some seriously grooving rock keyboard styles.

We'll jump straight into some basic piano "comping" (or accompaniment) patterns, explaining any necessary theory along the way. Then we'll add some voicing techniques and rhythmic patterns that are vital for the contemporary rock pianist. We'll also spotlight some world-famous rock keyboard artists, and see how to incorporate their vocabulary into your own music.

This book will also introduce you to rock keyboard soloing, with some important scales and patterns you can begin using right away. All of these comping and soloing techniques will help you to create your own piano parts on a variety of rock songs and progressions.

Five complete songs in various rock styles are included in the "Style File" chapter at the end of the book. Some of these examples include transcribed piano solos. Jam with the rhythm section on these tunes using the play-along tracks. This is a great way to develop your keyboard chops within these different rhythmic grooves. Good luck with playing your Rock Keyboard!

–Mark Harrison

About the Audio

You will find audio demonstrations of most of the music examples in the book. The solo piano tracks feature the left-hand piano part on the left channel, and the right-hand piano part on the right channel, for easy "hands separate" practice. The full band tracks feature the rhythm section on the left channel and the piano on the right channel, so that you can play along with the band. This is all designed to give you maximum flexibility when practicing. All the keyboard tracks were recorded using an acoustic piano sound, unless otherwise noted in the text.

About the Author

Mark Harrison is a professional keyboardist, composer/arranger, and music educator/author based in Los Angeles. He has worked with top musicians such as Jay Graydon (Steely Dan), John Molo (Bruce Hornsby band), Jimmy Haslip (Yellowjackets), and numerous others. Mark currently performs with his own contemporary jazz band (the Mark Harrison Quintet) as well as with the Steely Dan tribute band Doctor Wu. His TV music credits include *Saturday Night Live*, *The Montel Williams Show*, *American Justice*, *Celebrity Profiles*, *America's Most Wanted*, *True Hollywood Stories*, the British documentary program *Panorama*, and many others.

Mark taught at the renowned Grove School of Music for six years, instructing hundreds of musicians from all around the world. He currently runs a busy private teaching studio, catering to the needs of professional and aspiring musicians alike. His students include Grammy winners, hit songwriters, members of the Boston Pops and L.A. Philharmonic orchestras, and first-call touring musicians with major acts.

Mark's music instruction books are used by thousands of musicians in over 20 countries, and are recommended by the Berklee College of Music for all their new students. He has also written Master Class articles for *Keyboard* and *How to Jam* magazines, covering a variety of different keyboard styles and topics. For further information on Mark's musical activities, education products, and on-line lessons, please visit *www.harrisonmusic.com*.

CONTENTS

Chapter 1

WHAT IS ROCK MUSIC?

Rock music is a contemporary music style that first emerged in the 1960s, and then went on to become the dominant form of popular music throughout the world. It was originally formed from a combination of 1950s R&B and country music, and then absorbed influences from other styles such as folk and gospel. The basic essential elements of rock music are electric (amplified) guitar and bass, together with drums and vocals. Although piano and keyboards are not essential to creating the rock music sound, they are nonetheless prominently featured in many classic lineups and recordings.

Early forms of rock music were fairly simple and basic, with the American and British bands of the time influencing each other, notably including the British Invasion that hit the U.S. in the mid-1960s. From this time onward, rock music began to split into various sub-styles and genres. Some of the more important rock sub-styles to emerge are as follows:

Blues-Rock

British bands such as the Rolling Stones and the Yardbirds were influenced by American blues, in particular the Chicago blues sound of Muddy Waters' band. These bands helped create the blues-rock genre by combining blues songs and form with rock rhythms and instrumentation. This was further developed in the U.S. by artists such as Johnny Winter and Jimi Hendrix, and in the U.K. by bands like Cream, Led Zeppelin, and others. Subsequently, American bands such as Lynyrd Skynyrd and the Allman Brothers included country elements in their blues-rock, creating a sub-genre known as Southern Rock.

Notable blues-rock pianists and keyboardists include Chuck Leavell (Allman Brothers, Rolling Stones), Nicky Hopkins (The Who, Jeff Beck Group), and Ian Stewart (Rolling Stones, Led Zeppelin).

Classic Rock

Classic Rock began as a radio format, originating from the album-oriented rock styles that emerged in the 1970s. Today's Classic Rock radio stations generally feature music from the late-1960s to the mid-1980s, with an emphasis on 1970s recordings. Classic Rock is a rather broad category, and material from artists as diverse as the Beatles and Led Zeppelin can be heard on classic rock radio. Most classic rock songs are not hit singles, but have achieved considerable popularity as album tracks, generally with adult audiences. Certain 21st-century artists such as Sheryl Crow and Tom Petty produce what might be considered contemporary classic rock, as their music style fits in with these older songs. Because of this, their music is often included on classic rock radio playlists.

Notable classic rock pianists and keyboardists include David Paich (Toto, Michael Jackson), Roy Bittan (Bruce Springsteen, Dire Straits), and Benmont Tench (Tom Petty, U2).

Hard Rock

Hard rock is a derivation of blues-rock that began to emerge in the 1970s, reaching a peak in the late 1970s and early 1980s with bands such as AC/DC, Aerosmith, and Van Halen. This genre is characterized by high volume and intensity, often with repetitive riffs and distorted sounds from the electric guitar. Hard rock is also a fairly broad category, ranging from the classically influenced Deep Purple to the gothic overtones of Black Sabbath. This style in turn spawned a whole series of heavy metal bands from the 1980s onward, including Motorhead, Blue Oyster Cult, and Def Leppard.

Notable hard rock keyboardists include Jon Lord (Deep Purple), Dizzy Reed (Guns N' Roses), and Russ Irwin (Aerosmith).

Alternative Rock

Alternative rock was a term first applied to non-mainstream rock music in the 1980s, signifying a rejection of commercialism. Alternative rock became a staple of college radio playlists, and was often recorded for smaller, independent labels ("indies"). Most Alternative Rock bands were influenced by the punk-rock styles of the late 1970s. The style had a basic, stripped-down rock sound, delivered without showmanship or theatrics. Ironically, by the late 1980s Alternative rock bands such as R.E.M. and the Cure were enjoying considerable commercial success, and this style directly led to the hugely successful "grunge" rock bands of the 1990s, such as Nirvana and Pearl Jam. Alternative Rock is still going strong in the 21st century, with top-selling bands such as Train and Coldplay.

Notable alternative rock keyboardists include Mike Mills (R.E.M.), Roger O'Donnell (The Cure), and Brandon Bush (Train).

Pop/Rock

Pop/rock was created in the 1970s by combining the commercial melodies and accessible lyrics of pop music with the energy and drive of rock music. Early examples of this genre include Fleetwood Mac, Elton John, and Billy Joel. Pop/Rock reached a peak in the 1980s, with artists such as Phil Collins, Christopher Cross, and Hall & Oates enjoying great commercial success. Pop/rock artists from the 1990s then assimilated punk influences, including Blink-182, Green Day, and the Ben Folds Five. In the 2000s the Pop/Rock genre is continued by bands/artists such as Maroon 5, Kelly Clarkson, and Avril Lavigne.

As well as the above-mentioned Elton John, Billy Joel, and Ben Folds, other notable pop/rock keyboardists include Daryl Hall (Hall & Oates), Jeff Jacobs (Foreigner), and Mick MacNeil (Simple Minds). The multi-faceted pianist Bruce Hornsby expertly blends pop/rock stylings with country, R&B and jazz influences.

In Chapter 2, we'll get started with some basic comping patterns that you can use in rock songs. On with the show!

INTRO TO ROCK KEYBOARD COMPING

Left-Hand Quarter-Note Pattern

Our first rock keyboard pattern uses a steady quarter-note pulse in the left hand. A quarter-note lasts for one beat, so there are four "quarter-note beats" in a measure of 4/4 time, the most common time signature used in contemporary styles. This example plays the note G in the left hand, which is written on the bottom line of the bass clef, and is around one-and-a-half octaves below middle C. Note the "1, 2, 3, 4" written above the staff, which is how the beats are counted in 4/4 time:

TRACK 1

Listen to Track 1, and you can hear that the piano is on the right channel, and an accompanying rock rhythm section (bass and drums) is on the left channel. To hear the piano by itself, turn down the left channel; to play along with the band, turn down the right channel. Note the **repeat signs** used at the beginning and end of this example. This means that when we get to the end, we go back and repeat the example again, creating a four measure example in total. You should strive to play with rhythmic consistency and to lock in with the groove.

Next we're going to add a right-hand chord above this left-hand pattern. The first chords we'll work with in this book are **triads**, which are three-note chords. In this example we'll use a **G major triad**, consisting of the notes G, B, and D. A little theory note here: we can create a G major triad by taking the 1st, 3rd, and 5th degrees of a G major scale (which are G, B, and D). This creates **major 3rd** and **perfect 5th** intervals above G (i.e., G up to B is a major 3rd, and G up to D is a perfect 5th). More about the G major scale later on.

TRACK 2 TRACK 3
piano only piano plus
rhythm section

This is a two-handed example, written using the **grand staff**, a combination of treble and bass clefs. Note the "G" written above the treble clef. This is a **chord symbol**, and signifies that the chord being played is a G major chord. The left hand is playing the **root** of the chord (G), which is typical in rock piano styles. The right hand is playing whole-note triads. (Whole notes last for four beats.)

Listen to Track 2, and you can hear the left-hand part on the left channel, and the right-hand part on the right channel. To hear one hand's part by itself, just turn down one channel or the other. Then on Track 3, both the left-hand and right-hand piano parts are on the right channel, with the rhythm section on the left channel. To play along with the band, turn down the right channel. Again note that repeat signs are used, creating a four-measure phrase in total.

Left-Hand Eighth-Note Pattern

Our next pattern uses an eighth-note pulse in the left hand. We know a quarter-note lasts for one beat, so an eighth-note lasts for **half a beat**. This example again plays the note G in the left hand. Note the "1 & 2 & 3 & 4 &" written above the staff, which shows how rhythms using eighth notes are counted: the "&s" fall **halfway** between each beat, as follows:

TRACK 4

Rock piano players often emphasize the **downbeats** of the measure (the 1, 2, 3, and 4) by playing them a little harder than the **upbeats** (the "&s" between the downbeats). Next we'll add a G major triad above this pattern in the right hand:

TRACK 5   TRACK 6
piano only   piano plus
                rhythm section

Again notice that we are using whole-note G major triads in the right hand, and that the chord symbol "G" is shown above the staff. This left-hand rhythm is sometimes referred to as **straight eighths**, with each pair of eighth notes dividing the beat exactly in half.

Swing-Eighths (or Shuffle) Rhythmic Feel

Our next pattern uses a **swing-eighths** rhythm, sometimes referred to as a **shuffle**. Instead of dividing the beat exactly in half, the beat is now divided in a two-thirds/one-third ratio. In other words, the upbeat (or "&") is two-thirds of the way toward the next downbeat, rather than halfway. (Another theory note: This is equivalent to playing each pair of eighth notes as a quarter-note/eighth-note triplet. This is like a quarter note and an eighth note being proportionately "squeezed" into one beat.) Most often, swing-eighths music will be written the same way as straight-eighths, but with either a written description or symbol above the music indicating that the eighth notes are to be swung:

TRACK 7

Note this rhythm has a more "loping" feel compared to the straight-eighths example. We would still count this as "1 & 2 & 3 & 4 &," but the "&s" now come later during each beat. Practice this with the CD track until you are comfortable with this shuffle feel.

Next we'll add a G major triad above this swing-eighths pattern in the right hand:

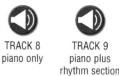

TRACK 8
piano only

TRACK 9
piano plus
rhythm section

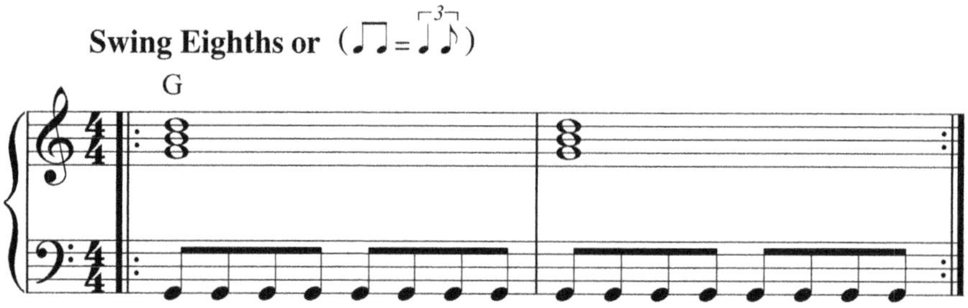

From now on in this book, we will use the description "swing eighths" above a music example if this rhythmic feel is to be used. However, bear in mind that the swing-eighths music symbol, shown above the last two examples, is also in common usage.

The I–IV–V Progression in the Key of C

Now it's time for us to work on our first **chord progression**, which is a sequence of chords used in a song. We'll have to cover a little more theory here, but I'll try to make it as painless as possible! If a chord progression is "in the key of C," this means that the note C is heard as the tonic or "home base," and that we are using notes within the C major scale. All major scales, including C major, can be built using a sequence of whole-step and half-step intervals:

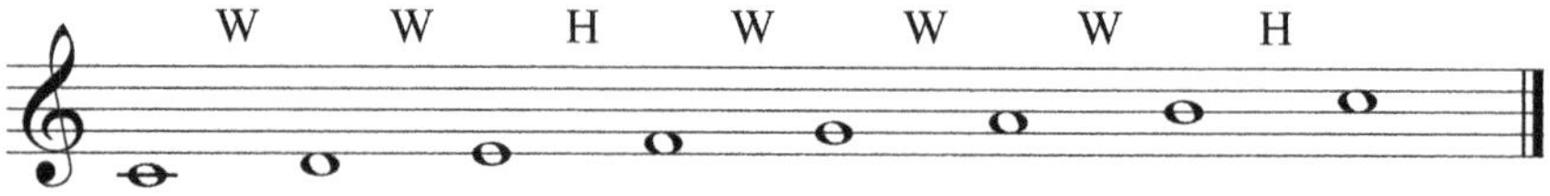

(See the Appendix at the back of this book for a list of all major scales).

A quick review of half-steps and whole-steps: a half-step is the distance from any note on the keyboard to the nearest note on the right or left (white and black keys included), and a whole-step is double the size of a half-step.

Music is normally written with a key signature on the left, which is a group of sharps or flats that lets you know which key you are in and which major scale to use. The key signature for C major is "no sharps and no flats," as none were needed when the scale was built using the above intervals (and starting on C).

(See the Appendix at the back of this book for a list of all key signatures).

We can then build triads—which, you remember, are three-note chords—from each note in this scale, while staying completely within the scale. The resulting triads are referred to as **diatonic triads**, as follows:

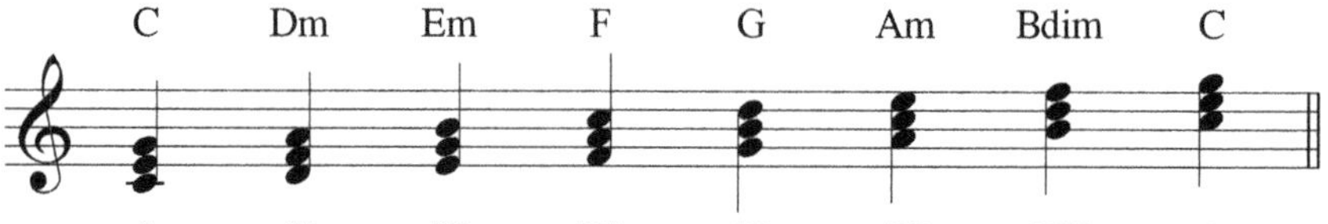

OK, just a few more things to explain here, then we'll get back to playing! Notice there are chord symbols above each of these diatonic triads in C major. We've already seen the "G" chord symbol before, which means a G major triad. Similarly, the "C" signifies a C major triad, and the "F" signifies an F major triad. We also have some symbols with an "m" suffix—Dm, Em, and Am. These are **minor triads**, which can be created by taking a major triad and "flatting" the 3rd (i.e., lowering it by a half-step). On the D minor chord this creates **minor 3rd** and **perfect 5th** intervals above D (i.e., D up to F is a minor 3rd, and D up to A is a perfect 5th). These intervals occur within all minor triads.

We also have a symbol with a "dim" suffix—Bdim. This is a **diminished triad**, which can be created by taking a major triad and "flatting" the 3rd and 5th. On the B diminished chord this creates **minor 3rd** and **diminished 5th** intervals above B (i.e., B up to D is a minor 3rd, and B up to F is a diminished 5th). Major and minor triads are widely used in rock styles, but the diminished triad is seldom used.

Note also that Roman numerals are shown below each chord, which indicates the **function** of each chord within the key. For example, in the key of C the C major triad is a I (or "one chord"), the D minor triad is a II (or "two chord") and so on. So now, when your band buddies ask you to play a "I–IV–V" progression in C, you'll know they want the C, F, and G major triads in a sequence! A lot of rock songs from different eras are based on this venerable chord progression. Take a look at this example:

Tracks 10/11 use the eighth-note left-hand pattern seen earlier, playing the **root** (fundamental tone) of each chord. For example, during the first measure the left hand is playing the bass note C during the C major chord, then during the second measure the left hand is playing the bass note F during the F major chord, and so on.

Notice that the right-hand triads are in **root position**, meaning that the root note is always the lowest note, and from bottom-to-top each triad is "voiced" with the root, 3rd, and 5th. For example, the C major triad in the first measure has the notes C-E-G from bottom-to-top. For beginning-level players, this is often the most comfortable, "default" way to play the chord. However, notice that while the above example sounds OK, the right-hand part jumps up between the C and F major triads, and then jumps back down again between the G and C major triads. These larger skips between chords can sound disjointed and unmusical in many style contexts.

Triad Inversions and Voice Leading

To solve this problem, we can use triad **inversions** and **voice leading**. A triad inversion occurs when we rearrange the notes of the chord, so that the root note is no longer on the bottom. Voice leading occurs when we move between successive chords smoothly, without the large interval skips in the previous example. The use of triad inversions means we can now voice lead between the chords in this progression:

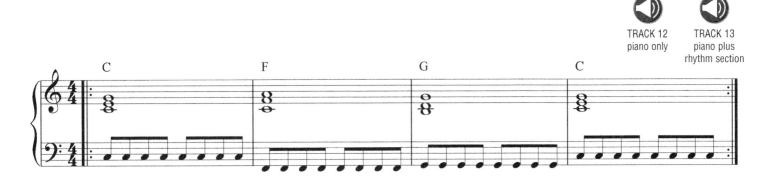

If you compare the first two measures in Tracks 12/13 to the first two measures in Tracks 10/11, you'll notice that the right-hand triad movement between C and F major is closer in Tracks 12/13 instead of the larger interval skip occurring in Tracks 10/11. This is because the F major triad is now in **second inversion**; the sequence of notes from bottom to top is now C-F-A, and the root of the chord (F) is now in the middle of the triad. Similarly, the G major triad in measure 3 above is now in **first inversion**; the sequence of notes from bottom to top is B-D-G, and the root of the chord (G) is now the top note of the triad. The use of these inversions, referred to as **voice leading**, gives a smooth, connected result when moving between the chords. Most rock styles, apart from basic hard rock and metal styles, will require the keyboard player to voice lead in this way when connecting between chords.

More Right-Hand Rhythm Patterns

So far we've been playing only whole note triads with the right hand. Now it's time to introduce more right-hand rhythms. A lot of the energy in piano rock styles comes from the rhythmic variations and "upbeats" in the right-hand part, combined with steady driving patterns in the left hand:

TRACK 14
piano only

TRACK 15
piano plus
rhythm section

The right-hand part in this example uses two-measure rhythmic phrases, a common device across a range of contemporary styles. In the first measure, the C major triad lands on beat 1, then halfway through beat 3 (on the "& of 3;" see rhythmic counting on Track 4). Then in the second measure, the F major triad lands halfway through beat 1 (on the "& of 1"), then on beat 3. This two-measure rhythmic phrase is then repeated during measures 3–4, over the G and C major chords. Meanwhile the left hand is again playing the root of each chord in a repeated eighth-note pattern, adding octaves to create a bigger, heavier sound.

The Classic Blues/Rock Left-Hand Pattern

Next we'll use the same right-hand part in a blues/rock style, by combining it with a classic left-hand pattern that you should know! This left-hand pattern alternates between the root-5th and root-6th of each chord. For example on a C chord, the note a 5th interval above the root is G, so the root-5th interval would be the notes C-G. Similarly, the note a 6th interval above the root is A, so the root-6th interval would be the notes C-A. So, the "root-5th, root-6th" pattern on this chord would alternate between the intervals C-G and C-A:

TRACK 16
piano only

TRACK 17
piano plus
rhythm section

Swing eighths

10

This example uses a swing-eighths or "shuffle" feel. (Review tracks 7–9 as needed.) Note that during the F major chord in measure 2, the left hand plays the root-5th, root-6th of F (i.e., F-C, F-D), and during the G major chord in measure 3, the left hand plays the root-5th, root-6th of G (i.e., G-D, G-E). This left-hand pattern works great on many blues and blues/rock songs.

More Chords and Rhythm Patterns in the Key of F

Now we're going to explore some keys other than C major. Let's derive the F major scale, using the same series of whole-step and half-step intervals that we used for C major, but this time starting on F:

Note that a B♭ is now needed in this scale, as this is the only way that we can get the necessary half-step above the preceding note (A). Next we'll derive the diatonic triads belonging to the F major scale:

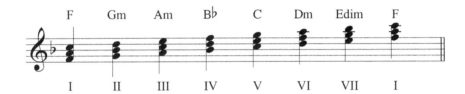

You'll notice that we have the key signature of F major shown on the left, the single flat sign. This reminds us that all occurrences of the note B in the music will be played as B♭. Also, seeing this key signature in the music will give us a heads-up that we are in the key of F.

Previously in the key of C, we have used a I–IV–V chord progression. However, there are of course many other diatonic chord progression possibilities! The next chord progression, in the key of F, is V–VI–IV–I, another typical sequence:

TRACK 18
piano only

TRACK 19
piano plus
rhythm section

Comparing this progression to the previous example showing all the diatonic triads in F major, we can see that the C–Dm–B♭–F sequence is a V–VI–IV–I (five, six, four, one) in this key. Note that we are again using triad inversions to voice lead smoothly from left to right, and we are again using a two-measure rhythmic phrase in the right hand. For example, in measure 1 the C major triad is played on beats 1 and 4, and then the D minor triad is played **ahead of** measure 2, actually landing halfway through beat 4 of measure 1 (on the "& of 4"), and "tied over" (extending into) measure 2. This is referred to as an **anticipation**, and is a staple technique in piano rock styles. Notice that the left hand is still landing on beat 1 of measure 2, playing D, the root of the D minor chord. This right-hand rhythmic pattern is then repeated during measures 3–4.

Meanwhile the left hand is playing a dotted-quarter/eighth/half pattern on the roots of the chords—i.e., playing a dotted quarter note (1-1/2 beats), followed by an eighth note (1/2 a beat), followed by a half note (2 beats). This is another common left-hand pattern in ballad and pop/rock piano styles.

More Chords and Rhythm Patterns in the Key of G

Next we'll derive the G major scale, again using the same series of whole-step and half-step intervals that we used for C and F major:

Note that an F♯ is needed in this scale, as this is the only way that we can get the necessary whole-step above the preceding note (E). Here are the diatonic triads belonging to the G major scale:

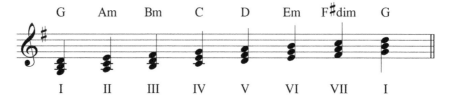

You'll notice that we have the key signature of G major shown on the left (the single sharp sign). This reminds us that all occurrences of the note F in the music will be played as F♯. Also, seeing this key signature in the music will give us a heads-up that we are in the key of G.

The next chord progression, in the key of G, is I–III–IV–I, again a typical sequence:

TRACK 20
piano only

TRACK 21
piano plus
rhythm section

Comparing this progression to the previous example showing all the diatonic triads in G major, we can see that the G–Bm–C–G sequence is a I–III–IV–I (one, three, four, one) in this key. Again, right-hand triad inversions and two-measure rhythmic phrases are being used. The left-hand pattern is a variation on the one used for Tracks 18/19, now with a root note added on beats 2 and 4 (the "backbeats"). This is played by the thumb, an octave higher than the roots played on beats 1 and 3 of the measure. This octave pattern and busier rhythm result in a driving, effective left-hand pattern, which is very useful in rock piano styles.

Rock Shuffle Comping Pattern in the Key of C

Now we'll return to the key of C, for a 50s-style rock shuffle comping pattern, using a swing-eighths feel:

TRACK 22
piano only

TRACK 23
piano plus
rhythm section

Comparing this example to the diatonic triads in C major, we can see that the C–Am–F–G sequence is I–VI–IV–V (one, six, four, five) in this key. This progression is a staple of many pop and rock songs, particularly from the 1950s and '60s. Again, right-hand triad inversions are being used, this time with a busier rhythm accenting the **upbeats** (halfway between each beat). The left hand is playing an eighth-note octave pattern, with the low root of each chord played with the pinky on the **downbeats** (i.e., beats 1, 2, 3, and 4 of each measure), and the same root note an octave higher played with the thumb on the **upbeats** in between.

Power Chord Voicings and Comping

Our last example in this chapter borrows the "power chord" voicing technique from guitar players. This involves playing just the root and 5th of the chord, rather than the root, 3rd, and 5th that we have been using so far. This gives a hollow, transparent feel to the chords:

TRACK 24
piano only

TRACK 25
piano plus
rhythm section

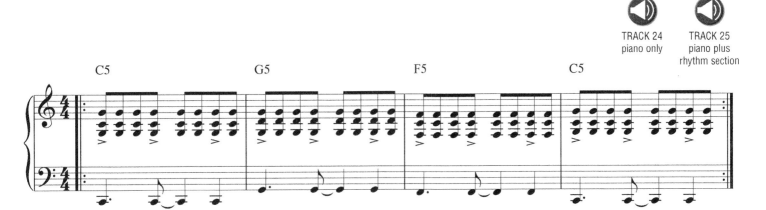

Note the chord symbols in this example, which have a "5" suffix— C5, G5, etc. This chord symbol suffix means "root and 5th only." Alternatively you may see symbols such as "C(omit3)" or "C(no3)," which mean the same thing. This progression is I–V–IV–I (one, five, four, one) in C, with each chord symbol modified to become a power chord. Note that we are still **voice leading** from left to right, selecting either the root or 5th of the chord for the top note in the right hand, to move smoothly from the previous chord. Each top note (either the root or 5th of the chord) is then doubled an octave lower with the right-hand thumb, adding more power and weight to the voicing. We can further analyze each right-hand voicing used:

Measure 1	The top note (G) is the 5th of the C major chord, and is placed above the root of the chord (C). The top note is then doubled an octave lower, creating a 5th-root-5th voicing (G-C-G from bottom to top) on the chord.
Measure 2	The top note (G) is now the root of the G major chord, and is placed above the 5th of the chord (D). The top note is then doubled an octave lower, creating a root-5th-root voicing (G-D-G from bottom to top) on the chord.
Measure 3	The top note (F) is the root of the F major chord, and is placed above the 5th of the chord (C). The top note is then doubled an octave lower, creating a root-5th-root voicing (F-C-F from bottom to top) on the chord.
Measure 4	Same as measure 1.

Rhythmically, the right-hand part is driving the pattern forward by playing on all of the eighth-note subdivisions, accenting beat one, halfway through beat 2 (the "& of 2"), and beat 4. This rhythm is also being played by the left hand, again following the roots of the chords. This type of power chord voicing is commonly used in harder rock and metal styles.

Chapter 3

MORE ROCK KEYBOARD VOICINGS AND PATTERNS

Right-Hand Arpeggios Using Eighth Notes

In this chapter we'll build on the foundation in Chapter 2 by adding lots more cool voicings and patterns that the rock keyboardist should know! We'll begin with triad **arpeggios** (broken chords). This involves playing the notes of a chord one-at-a-time instead of all together. Again this is a common guitar technique in pop and rock styles, which we can adapt for use on the keyboard. First we'll look at a chord progression in the key of F, which will be a good vehicle for this arpeggio technique:

TRACK 26
piano only

TRACK 27
piano plus
rhythm section

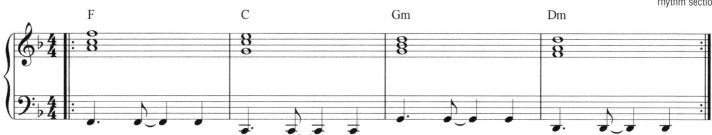

This is a simple pattern, voice leading between whole-note triads in the right hand, and supported by a rhythmic root note pattern in the left hand. The chord progression is I–V–II–VI (one, five, two, six) in the key of F. Review the diatonic triads in the key of F back in Chapter 2 if you're not sure about this! Now we'll apply a right-hand eighth-note arpeggio pattern to the above voicings:

TRACK 28
piano only

TRACK 29
piano plus
rhythm section

This pattern is reminiscent of the alternative rock anthem "Clocks" by Coldplay. Note that the right-hand arpeggio is created by playing the notes of the inverted F major triad in a descending sequence, and that the eight eighth-notes in each measure are split into a "3-3-2"-type pattern—i.e., in the first measure there are two decending three-note arpeggios (F-C-A), followed by a two-note figure (F-C). This creates a type of rhythmic displacement that is typical in pop and rock keyboard styles.

Right-Hand Arpeggios Using 16th Notes

Next we'll look at a **16th-note** arpeggio version of this chord progression in the key of F. In case you're not familiar with 16th-notes, they divide the beat into four parts (and divide the eighth note into two parts). Sixteenth notes create a more rhythmically intense effect than eighth notes, and are used in rock ballads at slower tempos, as well as up-tempo rock songs to add a funk/R&B influence. Here is the same chord progression, now using 16th note arpeggios in a rock ballad style:

TRACK 30
piano only

TRACK 31
piano plus
rhythm section

On Track 31, an electric organ part has been added to the bass and drums on the left channel.

The above arpeggios are mostly descending and use important rhythmic **anticipations**. As stated earlier, an anticipation occurs when a note or chord lands before the beat, and is then held through the following beat (or followed by a rest on that beat). In contemporary styles, anticipations will use either eighth or 16th notes, depending on the overall rhythmic subdivision of the style. For example, in Tracks 24–29 the left-hand pattern anticipates beat 3 of each measure by an eighth note. In the above example, the right-hand arpeggios anticipate beat 3 by a 16th note. Using anticipations in this way is a critical element to making the groove happen! Meanwhile the left hand is simply playing the roots of the chords in the above example, as half notes landing on beats 1 and 3 of each measure. This simple pattern is an effective support to the busier right-hand figures.

Note the sustain pedal markings that require the sustain pedal to be depressed for the duration of each chord. This helps to create a fuller sound and is generally required for all piano ballad styles. (For more up-tempo rock, however, the pedal should be used sparingly, if at all, because it can detract from the rhythmic drive needed.)

You remember that back in Chapter 2 we counted eighth-note rhythms as "1 & 2 & 3 & 4 &." Well, if we want to count 16th-note rhythms, we'll have to add something between the "1" and the "&," and between the "&" and "2," and so on. This is done by using the syllables "e" and "a," as in "1 e & a 2 e & a," etc. More about 16th-note figures (and counting) later on!

Four-Part Chords in the Key of C

As we have seen, triads (three-part chords) are widely used in rock keyboard styles. But what happens if we want a larger, denser chordal sound in a song? Well, then we could use **four-part** chords, which have four different notes in them. These are sometimes referred to as **seventh chords**, as most of them contain a seventh interval between the root and a chord tone.

Back in Chapter 2, we built **diatonic triads** from each note in a C major scale. Now we'll build diatonic four-part chords from each note in this scale, again staying completely within the scale:

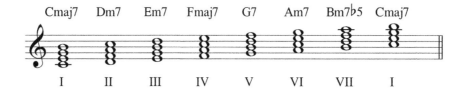

OK, time for some more theory. Notice there are chord symbols above each of these diatonic four-part chords in C major:

- The symbols with the "maj7" suffix are major seventh chords, which can be created by taking a major triad and adding the note that is a major 7th interval above the root (equivalent to the 7th degree of the major scale built from the root). On the C major 7th chord, this means we have major 3rd, perfect 5th, and major 7th intervals above the root C. The same interval pattern also occurs in the Fmaj7 chord.

- The symbols with the "m7" suffix are minor seventh chords, which can be created by taking a minor triad and adding the note that is a minor 7th interval above the root (equivalent to the 7th degree of the major scale built from the root, lowered by half-step). On the D minor 7th chord, this means we have minor 3rd, perfect 5th, and minor 7th intervals above the root D. The same interval pattern also occurs in the Em7 and Am7 chords.

- The symbol with the "7" suffix is a dominant seventh chord, which can be created by taking a major triad and adding the note that is a minor 7th interval above the root (equivalent to the 7th degree of the major scale built from the root, lowered by half-step). On the G (dominant) 7th chord, this means we have major 3rd, perfect 5th, and minor 7th intervals above the root G.

- The symbol with the "m7♭5" suffix is a minor seventh with flatted 5th chord, which can be created by taking the minor seventh chord and flatting the 5th by a half-step. This chord is also referred to as a "half-diminished seventh" chord.

Major, minor, and dominant seventh chords are commonly used in pop, rock, and R&B styles, but the "minor 7th with flatted 5th" chord is seldom used. (This is more of a jazz sound.)

As for the diatonic triads in Chapter 2, note that Roman numerals are again shown below each chord, indicating the **function** of each chord within the key. For example, in the key of C, the C major seventh chord is a **I** (or "one chord"), the D minor seventh chord is a **II** (or "two chord"), and so on. Our next example is a pop/rock shuffle using some of these four-part chords, in the key of C:

Swing eighths

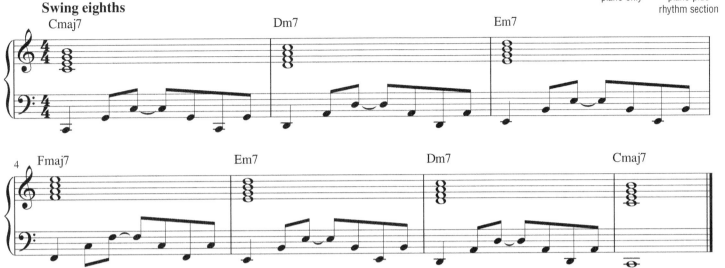

Here the right hand is playing whole-note four-part chords in root position (i.e., with the root note on the bottom) over a left-hand pattern that uses the root and 5th of each chord and anticipates beat 3 in each measure. The harmony and rhythms of this example are reminiscent of 1960s Motown styles.

Four-Part Chord Inversions and Voice Leading

Even though we were using only root position chords in the previous example, the voice leading (moving smoothly between chords) was still pretty good, because the progression was moving up and down the diatonic series (i.e., from a I chord, to a II chord, to a III chord, etc.). However, for most other types of four-part chord progressions, we will need to use inversions to voice lead correctly between the chords, just like we did with triad progressions in Chapter 2. The next example uses inversions to voice lead between a I–IV–II–VI (one, four, two, six) four-part chord progression in C:

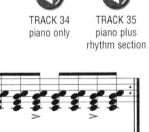
TRACK 34
piano only

TRACK 35
piano plus
rhythm section

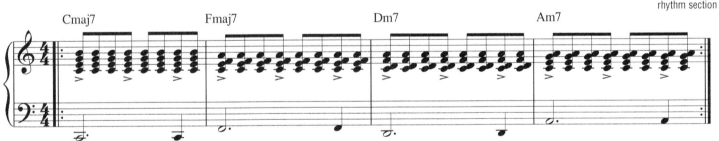

The right-hand rhythmic accents in this example are similar to Tracks 24/25: accenting beat one, halfway through beat 2 (the "& of 2"), and beat 4. The left hand is supporting this pattern by playing the chord roots on beats 1 and 4 of each measure.

In general, using these four-part chords in the right hand creates a denser, more sophisticated sound (compared to using triads). For more basic rock styles, however, the simplicity and clarity of triads will be preferred. Let your ears be the judge! Also, it is possible to create/imply larger chords while still using triads in the right hand, as we are about to see.

Triad-Over-Root Chord Voicings

As an alternative to playing larger chords (such as four-part chords) in the right hand, we can split the chord so that the root is still played by the left hand, but the "upper part" is played by the right hand. Typically, this upper part forms a triad, but functionally it is part of a larger chord. For example, if we take the Am7 four-part chord:

and split it so that the root note (A) is in the bass clef, and the remaining notes (C, E, G) are in the treble clef, it will look like the first chord in the following example:

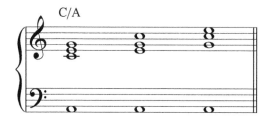

You'll recognize that these upper notes (C, E, G) spell a C major triad in their own right, which is why you see the **slash chord** symbol C/A (meaning "C major triad over the root note A") above the staff. However, while C/A is a perfectly valid chord symbol, it is not widely used in actual practice. You are much more likely to see Am7 written for this chord. Therefore it's useful to know that you can voice the A minor 7th chord by placing a C triad over the root of A. In other words, you are building a C major triad from the 3rd of the Am7 chord. This type of "triad-over-root" voicing has been a staple of pop/rock styles from the 1980s onward.

Another useful aspect of this triad-over-root voicing is that the upper triad (C major in this case) can be used in any inversion (for melodic or voice leading purposes). All inversions of the upper C major triad are shown in the above example. Next we'll look a Cmaj7 four-part chord, and derive a triad-over-root voicing:

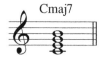

Now we'll split it so that the root note (C) is in the bass clef, and the remaining notes (E, G, B) are in the treble clef:

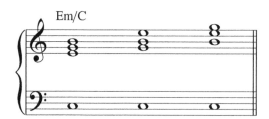

You can see that the upper notes (E, G, B) spell an E minor triad in their own right, which is why you see the chord symbol Em/C (meaning "E minor triad over the root note C") above the staff. Again, though, the symbol Em/C is not widely used in practice, so it's good to know that you can voice the Cmaj7 chord by building an E minor triad from the 3rd of the chord. The upper E minor triad is shown in all inversions.

Next we'll use these new triad-over-root voicings on a chord progression in a pop/rock style:

TRACK 36
piano only

TRACK 37
piano plus
rhythm section

The slash chord symbols are shown, to illustrate the triad-over-root voicings used. Harmonically, the first four measures can be analyzed as follows:

Measure 1   The upper C major triad has been built from the 3rd of the overall A minor 7th chord.

Measure 2   The upper E minor triad has been built from the 3rd of the overall C major 7th chord.

Measure 3   The upper F major triad has been built from the 3rd of the overall D minor 7th chord.

Measure 4   The upper A minor triad has been built from the 3rd of the overall F major 7th chord.

As you're more likely to see the chord symbols written as "Am7, Cmaj7, Dm7, Fmaj7" in practice, it's good to know which "upper triads" to use in response to these chord symbols. You've already heard this technique at work on many famous pop/rock recordings!

Alternating Triad Chord Voicings

Whereas triad-over-root voicings use a **single** upper triad over the root in the bass, "alternating triads" alternate between **two** upper triads over the root in the bass. This gives more motion and movement to the sound, and can be useful in pop/rock and blues/rock styles. Our first alternating triad example moves between the I and IV triads on a major chord (C and F major triads, over a C major chord):

TRACK 38
piano only

TRACK 39
piano plus
rhythm section

On Track 39, an electric organ part has been added to the bass and drums on the left channel.

This particular alternating triad technique—moving between the I and IV triads over a major chord—is sometimes referred to as **backcycling,** and is a staple of piano rock, blues, and gospel styles. In the first two measures, the right hand is playing the C major triad on beats 1 and 3 (the "strong" beats), alternating with the F major triad on beats 2 and 4 (the "weak" beats). These triads are then split into eighth-note pairs during measures 3 and 4, with the upper notes of each triad played on the **downbeats** (1, 2, 3, and 4), and the lowest note of each triad played by the thumb on all the **upbeats** (the "&s" in between). We'll see a similar right-hand technique used in eighth-note ballad styles later on. Meanwhile the left hand is playing the root-5th/root-6th pattern we heard earlier on Tracks 16/17. This all combines to create a classic bues/rock piano comping groove, which you can use on many different songs!

Our next alternating triad example is in more of a modern pop/rock vein, this time using a mix of major and minor chords:

TRACK 40
piano only

TRACK 41
piano plus
rhythm section

OK, it's time for a little more theory. You remember that on Tracks 36/37 we placed an F major triad over D in the bass, to voice a D minor 7th chord. (The F major triad was built from the 3rd of the Dm7 chord.) Well, the F major triad also appears in the first and last measures above (with the Dm7 chord symbol), now alternating with a C major triad. This C major triad can be thought of as being built from the 7th of the Dm7 chord. So, in total, we are alternating between triads built from the 7th (C) and from the 3rd (F) of the Dm7 chord during these measures. This can be referred to as "♭VII–♭III" alternating triads on the Dm7 chord, signifying that the roots of the upper triads are a **minor 7th** interval and a **minor 3rd** interval above the root of D, respectively. This device became a classic pop/rock keyboard sound from the 1980s onward, and is associated with artists such as the Doobie Brothers, Kenny Loggins, Christopher Cross, and numerous others.

During the second measure, the same C and F major triads are now being used on the F major chord (i.e., over the F in the bass), and this can be referred to as "V–I" alternating triads on the F major chord, as the C major triad is built from the 5th of the F major chord, and the F major triad is of course built from the root of the chord. Famous examples of V–I alternating triads occur at the beginning of the *Hill Street Blues* TV theme, and during the intro to Van Halen's classic rock anthem "Jump." During the third measure, we are again using ♭VII–♭III alternating triads, this time on the Gm7 chord, with F and B♭ major upper triads, respectively. Note that the first B♭ major triad in the right hand falls halfway through beat 4 of the previous measure (measure 2). This right-hand triad anticipation also prepares the harmony, since the B♭ upper hand belongs to the next chord.

In total, then, we can summarize the alternating triad voicings used in this example as follows:

Measure 1	The upper C and F major triads have been built from the 7th and 3rd of the overall D minor 7th chord, respectively. This is a ♭VII–♭III alternating triad pair.
Measure 2	The upper C and F major triads have been built from the 5th and root of the overall F major chord, respectively. This is a V–I alternating triad pair.
Measure 3	The upper F and B♭ major triads have been built from the 7th and 3rd of the overall G minor 7th chord, respectively. This is a ♭VII–♭III alternating triad pair.
Measure 4	Same as measure 1.

Rhythmically, the left hand is using the same octave pattern that we first heard on Tracks 20/21, again following the roots of the chords. This is a favorite pop/rock left-hand pattern, creating a good foundation below the right-hand rhythmic phrases and anticipations.

Rock Ballad Comping Using 16th Notes

Now it's time to further develop 16th-note patterns that can be used on rock ballads. Back on Tracks 30/31 we began to use 16th-note arpeggios in a rock ballad style. Now we'll combine right-hand triad voicings (playing three notes at once) with intervals (two notes at once) and arpeggios (single notes of the chord) to create a fuller texture:

TRACK 42
piano only

TRACK 43
piano plus
rhythm section

On Track 43, an electric organ part has been added to the bass and drums on the left channel.

This progression is I–IV–V–I in the key of C, and again uses inverted triads to voice lead smoothly between the chords in the right hand. On beat 1 of each measure, the full triad (all three notes) is played by the right hand. Then during beat 2 the triad is split, with the bottom note played halfway through beat 2, and the remaining notes of the triad on the last 16th note of beat 2, anticipating beat 3. Then during beat 4 the bottom two notes of the triad are arpeggiated (played as single notes) in a descending sequence. This is all supported by a steady quarter-note octave pattern in the left hand. Note the pedal markings, indicating that the sustain pedal should be depressed for the duration of each chord.

The next 16th-note rock ballad example adds chord inversions and rhythmic "pickups" in the left-hand part, as well as busier arpeggios in the right-hand part. You know that triad inversions occur when the notes of the triad are rearranged so that the root note is no longer on the bottom. So far, though, even when we have used triad inversions in the right hand, we have always played the root of the chord in the left hand. Now it's time to vary that by taking another note from the chord (normally either the 3rd or 5th, in pop and rock styles) and playing it in the left hand, instead of the normal root of the chord. This can be referred to as using "inversions in the bass," as in the following example:

TRACK 44
piano only

TRACK 45
piano plus
rhythm section

On Track 45, an electric guitar part has been added to the bass and drums on the left channel.

Compare the chord symbols in the above example to Tracks 42/43, and you'll notice the above example has F/A (instead of F) during measure 2, and G/B (instead of G) during measure 3. The F/A chord symbol means "place an F major triad over A in the bass," and as A is the 3rd of the F major chord, we can say that this chord is now "inverted over its 3rd." Although this type of **slash chord** symbol looks similar to those used in Tracks 36/37, it is in fact structurally different: the F/A and G/B chords are **inversions** over their respective 3rds, whereas the chords in Tracks 36/37 are **upper structure** voicings. For example, on the C/A chord, the C major triad contained the "upper notes" of an A minor 7th chord.

So why would we use these types of "inversions in the bass"? They give us a different vertical quality on the chord, and they can enable the bass line to move in a more melodic or step-wise manner during a song. In the above example, during measures 2–4 the left hand bass line moves from A-B-C as a result of the inversions in the bass, which is a pleasing step-wise movement within the C major scale.

Also in the above example, the right hand arpeggiates two triad tones during beat 2 of each measure, before playing the whole triad on the last 16th-note of beat 2, anticipating beat 3. The left-hand part is similar to Tracks 42/43, with an extra 16th note added at the end of each measure that functions as a pickup into the following chord. This helps to add more forward motion and energy to the groove!

Pop/Rock Comping Using Suspended Chords

Next we'll take a look at suspended chords, which are very important in rock keyboard styles. A suspended triad occurs when the 3rd of the chord is replaced with another note:

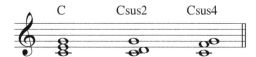

In this example, the C major triad is shown on the left, followed by the new **Csus2** and **Csus4** chord symbols:

- The **Csus2** symbol means "take the C major triad and replace the 3rd (E) with the 2nd degree in the C major scale (D)." The note D is also technically a 9th with respect to the root of C.

- The **Csus4** symbol means "take the C major triad and replace the 3rd (E) with the 4th degree in the C major scale (F)." The note F is also technically an 11th with respect to the root of C.

A word of clarification: if you encounter the chord symbol **Csus**, then **Csus4** is assumed. This is the most common type of suspension.

Like regular triads, suspended triads can be inverted and voice-led during progressions. Here's a pop/rock keyboard example using suspended triads, reminiscent of the pop/rock duo Hall & Oates:

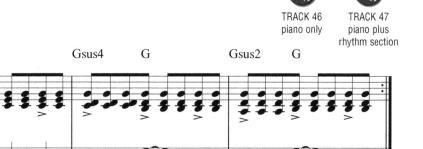

On Track 47, an electric guitar part has been added to the bass and drums on the left channel.

This example is rhythmically similar to Tracks 24/25 and 34/35, now using the suspensions to create inner motion and interest within the chords. Note that all the G major and suspended triads in measures 3–4 are inverted, with the note G on top, to voice lead smoothly from the previous two measures.

Mixolydian 3rd Intervals and Patterns

Now it's time to unlock the mysteries of the **Mixolydian mode**, an important "secret weapon" in the rock keyboardist's arsenal! Here is the G Mixolydian mode, which contains all the white keys from G up to the next G on the keyboard:

Another little theory note: the term "Mixolydian mode" technically means "a major scale displaced to start on its 5th degree." If we take the C major scale derived back in Chapter 2, and start the scale on its 5th degree (G), we will get the G Mixolydian mode above. Another way to construct a Mixolydian mode is to take a major scale and lower the 7th degree by half-step. If we take the G major scale derived back in Chapter 2 and lower the 7th degree by half-step (i.e., replace the F♯ with F), we will again get the G Mixolydian mode above.

(See the Appendix at the back of this book, for a list of all Mixolydian modes.)

Rock keyboard players love to use this mode when playing over **dominant 7th chords**, which are a staple of blues/rock harmony. Earlier in this chapter, you'll remember that we derived all the four-part diatonic chords in the key of C, including the G7 dominant chord built from the 5th degree of the scale. Well, if you look at the G Mixolydian mode and take the 1st, 3rd, 5th, and 7th notes, these are G, B, D, and F. Collectively, they spell the G7 chord. This chord is therefore contained within the G Mixolydian mode, which can then be referred to as a "scale source" for this chord.

One common application of Mixolydian modes is to extract 3rd intervals and use them in a comping pattern. Here are the 3rd intervals contained within the G Mixolydian mode:

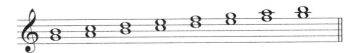

Now we'll build some patterns using the B-D, C-E, and D-F intervals shown above, for use on a G7 dominant chord:

TRACK 48
piano only

TRACK 49
piano plus
rhythm section

Looking at the right-hand part in this example, we see the Mixolydian 3rd intervals (B-D, C-E, D-F, and C-E) being used on all the downbeats (i.e., beats 1, 2, 3, and 4) in each measure. The use of the B-D and D-F intervals on beats 1 and 3 is important, as these intervals are most "inside" the G7 chord, and are therefore placed on beats 1 and 3, the strong beats in a 4/4 measure. The C-E intervals on beats 2 and 4 are passing intervals (placed on the weak beats) that connect between the other intervals on the strong beats. Meanwhile, the right-hand thumb is playing the root (G) on all of the upbeats. Harmonically, this example is similar to Tracks 38/39, which alternated between I and IV triads on the strong and weak beats, respectively.

During measures 3–4 the right-hand part is using half-step **grace notes** to lead into the 3rd (B) and 5th (D) of the implied G7 chord. These are ornamental notes of short duration, which are squeezed in right before the following note. For example, on beat 1 of measure 3, the A♯ is squeezed in right before the B and D that follow. (Actually, although it looks like we should play the A♯ by itself and then play the B and D together afterward, in practice the blues-rock keyboardist **plays the A♯ and D together**, then quickly slides off the A♯ to play the B afterward.)

Meanwhile, the left hand is playing a "root-5th, root-6th, root-7th, root-6th" pattern on the G7 chord. This is similar to other blues-rock left-hand patterns we have seen, except that we are using quarter notes instead of eighth notes, and the left-hand thumb is playing the 7th of the chord on beat 3 of each measure. Since the right hand is playing on all of the eighth-note subdivisions, the left hand can get away with playing only on the quarter notes—i.e., the left hand doesn't need to play on all the eighth notes.

Now we'll put this "Mixolyian 3rd interval" pattern to work—this time without the grace notes—on a complete 12-bar blues progression, in the key of C:

TRACK 50
piano only

TRACK 51
piano plus
rhythm section

This example uses Mixolydian modes built from the root of each chord, as a basis for the 3rd interval patterns. You'll recognize the G Mixolydian mode (the 3rd intervals B-D, C-E, and D-F) being used on the G7 chords in measures 9 and 12. Similarly, the C Mixolydian mode (the 3rd intervals E-G, F-A, and G-B♭) is being used on the C7 chords in measures 1, 3–4, 7–8 and 11. The F Mixolydian mode (the 3rd intervals A-C, B♭-D, and C-E♭) is being used on the F7 chords in measures 2, 5–6, and 10. The left-hand pattern is again based on the root-5th, root-6th, and root-7th of each chord, now using an eighth-note subdivision.

This is also our first example of a 12-bar blues progression, which is a form commonly used in blues and blues-rock styles. This 12-bar form contains three four-measure phrases, which normally start with chords built from the 1st, 4th, and 5th scale degrees of the key, respectively. The blues form does not normally use diatonic chords, instead favoring dominant 7th chords built from each of these scale degrees (i.e., using C7, F7, and G7 chords on a blues progression in C).

Unison Riffs Using the Minor Pentatonic Scale

In rock styles, a riff is a short melodic phrase, usually one to four measures in length, played on guitar and/or keyboard, which is repeated as part of the structure or arrangement of the song. Rock riffs are often played by the guitar, bass, and keyboard in unison (i.e., playing the same notes at the same time). If the keyboardist is playing a riff with both hands, the left hand usually doubles the right-hand figure, one or more octaves lower. Two of the most common sources for rock riffs are the **minor pentatonic scale** and its close cousin, the **blues scale**.

OK, time for a little more theory. First we'll derive the **pentatonic scale** (sometimes referred to as the **major pentatonic scale**), then we'll use this to derive the **minor pentatonic** and **blues scales**. We can derive a pentatonic scale by taking a major scale and removing the 4th and 7th degrees, as in this C pentatonic scale:

Comparing this to the C major scale we derived in Chapter 2, notice that the 4th and 7th scale degrees (F and B) have been removed. The pentatonic scale is widely used in country and New Age styles, among others. Now if we displace this scale to start on the note A, the 6th degree of the C major scale, we get the A minor pentatonic scale:

(See the Appendix at the back of this book for a list of all pentatonic and minor pentatonic scales.)

The sixth degree of the major scale, A in the C major scale, is significant in that it is the **relative minor** of the major scale. In other words, we can say that "A minor is the relative minor of C major." The relative minor key shares the same key signature as the major key, so the key signature for C major (no sharps and no flats) that we derived in Chapter 2 also works for the key of A minor. Similarly, the key signature for F major (one flat) also works for the key of D minor (as D is the sixth degree of the F major scale), and so on.

We could therefore say that the above A minor pentatonic scale was derived by taking the C pentatonic scale and starting it on the **relative minor**, in this case the note A. Now it's time to create an eighth-note rock riff using the A minor pentatonic scale:

TRACK 52
piano only

TRACK 53
piano plus
rhythm section

On Track 53, an electric guitar part has been added to the bass and drums on the left channel.

In the above example, the left hand is doubling (duplicating) the right-hand part, one octave lower. Note that within the four-measure phrase, there are two two-measure phrases that start in a similar way but end differently (i.e., measures 1 and 3 are similar, but measures 2 and 4 are different). This is typical of rock riff phrasing, and of contemporary style phrasing in general.

Unison Riffs Using the Blues Scale

Now if we take the A minor pentatonic scale and add a half-step connector between the notes D and E, we get an A blues scale:

(See the Appendix at the back of this book, for a list of all blues scales.)

The A blues scale is similar to the A minor pentatonic scale, with just one extra note (D♯/E♭). This is an important additional note, however, giving us the half-steps in the middle of the scale that are characteristic of the blues. Next we'll create a 16th-note rock riff using this A blues scale, reminiscent of the classic rock band Led Zeppelin:

TRACK 54
piano only

TRACK 55
piano plus
rhythm section

On Track 55, an electric guitar part has been added to the bass and drums on the left channel.

In the above example, the left hand is again doubling the right-hand part, and the four-measure phrase structure is similar to the example in Tracks 52/53, but now with a 16th-note subdivision. Rock on!

Chapter 4

ROCK KEYBOARD COMPING STYLES

In this chapter we'll spotlight four of the most important and influential rock keyboardists of all time: Billy Joel, Elton John, Bruce Hornsby, and Ben Folds. Through comping examples based on some of their best-known songs, we'll get to see and hear what makes their particular styles tick, and how to apply these tools and techniques to your own music.

Billy Joel

Billy Joel has been a major influence on many keyboardists and songwriters from the 1970s onward, with piano styles that range from tender ballads to hard-driving rock songs. Our first Billy Joel-influenced comping example is in the style of his classic mid-tempo pop song "Just the Way You Are," recorded with an electric piano sound:

Comping example #1 — Style of "Just the Way You Are" by Billy Joel

TRACK 56
piano only

TRACK 57
piano plus
rhythm section

On Track 57, an electric organ part has been added to the bass and drums on the left channel.

In the first eight measures of this example, the right hand is playing a mix of arpeggios and triads. For example, in measure 1 the D major triad in second inversion is arpeggiated (A-D-F♯ from bottom to top), leading to a G triad in first inversion landing halfway through beat 2 (and anticipating beat 3). Note also the use of **triad-over-root** voicings on the Bm7, Gmaj7, and Em7 chords. Meanwhile, in this section the left hand is anchoring the root with a simple half-note pattern.

Then beginning in measure 9, the energy builds when the left hand switches to a dotted-quarter/eighth/half-note pattern, again playing the root of each chord, with the right-hand triads anticipating beat 1 by an eighth note. This is typical of Billy Joel's style, and of pop/rock keyboard styles in general.

The next comping example is in the style of "My Life," which shows Billy Joel's up-tempo pop/rock side:

Comping example #2 – Style of "My Life" by Billy Joel

TRACK 58
piano only

TRACK 59
piano plus
rhythm section

On Track 59, an electric guitar part has been added to the bass and drums on the left channel.

Note the hard-driving left-hand octave pattern that underpins this example. The right hand is using various alternating triad techniques:

Measures 1–4, 11–13:   IV – I (B♭ to F) and V - I (C to F) alternating triads over the F major chord.

Measures 7–8:   V – I (F to B♭) alternating triads over the B♭ major chord.

Measures 9–10:   IV – I (F to C) alternating triads over the C major chord.

In total, the alternating triads used are the I, IV, and V (F, B♭, and C) of the key (F major). This overall diatonic restriction often applies in harmonically simpler pop/rock styles. The F/A chord in measure 6 is an example of a major triad inverted over its 3rd in the bass, enabling the bass note (A) to move smoothly by half-step to the root of the next chord (B♭).

Our final Billy Joel-influenced comping example is in the style of his famous pop/rock shuffle "It's Still Rock 'n' Roll to Me," again recorded with an electric piano sound:

Comping example #3 – Style of "It's Still Rock 'n' Roll to Me" by Billy Joel

TRACK 60
piano only

TRACK 61
piano plus
rhythm section

The secret to playing this up-tempo shuffle groove is to place the swing-eighths subdivisions correctly during beats 3 and 4 of each measure, in the right hand. For example, in measure 1 the G major triad will land **two-thirds** of the way into beat 3 (not just halfway, as would be the case with straight eighths). Similarly, the single note D is landing two-thirds of the way into beat 4; this is part of the D major triad that is an upper structure triad-over-root voicing on the following Bm7 chord.

The left hand is providing a solid foundation below these right-hand upbeats, playing the root of each chord in a steady quarter-note pattern. This is typical of faster pop/rock shuffle styles, where playing a swing-eighths pattern in the left hand at this tempo might be too busy or distracting.

Elton John

Like Billy Joel, Elton John's work runs the gamut from ballads to muscular rock songs. His style also shows significant gospel and R&B influences. Our first Elton John-influenced comping example is in the style of his classic mid-tempo anthem "Sad Songs":

Comping example #4 – Style of "Sad Songs" by Elton John

TRACK 62
piano only

TRACK 63
piano plus
rhythm section

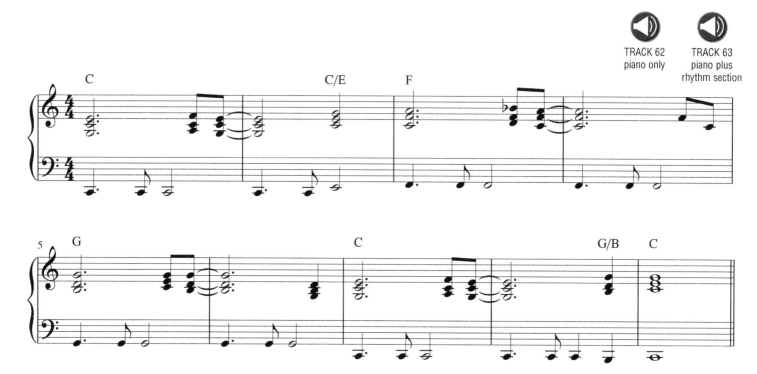

On Track 63, an electric guitar part has been added to the bass and drums on the left channel.

This is a good example of the use of IV–I alternating triads in a rock song. Note that on the C major chord in measures 1 and 7, we move from a first inversion F major triad (on beat 4) to a second inversion C major triad (halfway through beat 4, anticipating beat 1 of the next measure). Similarly, we are moving between B♭ and F major triads on the F major chord in measure 3, and between C and G major triads on the G major chord in measure 5. Also note the C/E and G/B chords in measures 2 and 8 respectively. These are major triads inverted over their 3rds, again enabling the left-hand root note to move up by half-step into the root of the next chord.

Meanwhile, the left hand is playing a steady dotted-quarter/eighth/half-note rhythmic pattern, which works for a variety of tempos, from ballads to mid- and up-tempo rock songs.

The next comping example is in the style of "I'm Still Standing," a classic pop/rock song with a swing-eighths subdivision at a faster tempo:

Comping example #5 – Style of "I'm Still Standing" by Elton John

TRACK 64
piano only

TRACK 65
piano plus
rhythm section

On Track 65, a synthesizer pad (chordal part) has been added to the bass and drums on the left channel.

The rhythmic style of this example is similar to example #3 (Tracks 60/61), with a steady quarter-note pulse in the left hand, below right-hand triads that anticipate the following downbeat. Again, make sure you place the right-hand triads two-thirds of the way through beat 4 of each measure. Beginning in measure 9, the right hand adds arpeggios that start on beat 3 of the odd-numbered measures, increasing the energy level in this section.

This example also uses a bass pedal tone, a repeated bass note below different upper triads: in measures 1–4, the bass note A is played in the left hand below the upper triads Am, Dm, G, and Am. Also, for extra power and emphasis the left hand is playing mostly the quarter-note pattern in octaves. This is typical of Elton John's style.

Our final Elton John-influenced comping example is in the style of his famous rock ballad "Little Jeannie," recorded with an electric piano sound:

Comping example #6 – Style of "Little Jeannie" by Elton John

On Track 67, an electric organ part has been added to the bass and drums on the left channel.

This example is a 16th-note rock ballad. As you can see, 16th-note subdivisions are used in the right-hand part, during beats 3 and 4 of the odd-numbered measures. In these bars the right hand plays a triad on beat 3, followed by a 16th-note arpeggio pattern that anticipates beat 4 by a 16th note. This leads to another triad that anticipates beat 1 of the next measure and belongs to it harmonically.

This example also contains some triads inverted over their 3rds in the bass: the D/F♯ chord in measures 2 and 6, and the C/E chord in measures 4 and 8. The left hand is using partial arpeggio patterns, playing the root-5th-root of the G and F major chords, and the 3rd-root-3rd of the D/F♯ and C/E chords. These patterns leave plenty of space in the latter half of these measures, for the right-hand triads and 16th notes. In measure 9 the left hand changes to a root-5th pattern using quarter notes, on the B♭ and C major chords. These devices are typical of Elton John's R&B-influenced rock ballad style.

Bruce Hornsby

To call Bruce Hornsby a rock pianist is almost misleading. He is a stylistic chameleon who effortlessly blends rock, jazz, country, gospel, and jam-band influences to create a unique style. However, his rock piano chops are formidable, and in this section we'll focus on examples in the style of some of his best-known rock songs. Our first Bruce Hornsby-influenced comping example is in the style of his classic mid-tempo rocker "The Way It Is":

Comping example #7 – Style of "The Way It Is" by Bruce Hornsby

TRACK 68
piano only

TRACK 69
piano plus
rhythm section

On Track 69, an electric guitar part has been added to the bass and drums on the left channel.

In measures 1–4 of this example, both hands are playing the same rhythms. In measures 1–3 we are landing on beat 1 and halfway through beat 2, anticipating beat 3 by an eighth note. In measure 4 both hands are simply playing whole notes. The voicings include some **triad-over-root** chords in measure 1 (the C major triad built from the 3rd of the Am7 chord, and the G major triad built from the 3rd of the Em7 chord), and a **suspended** chord in measure 4. (We saw in Chapter 3 that the Csus2 chord was derived by replacing the note E with D within a C major triad.) These triad-over-root and suspended voicings are a vital part of Bruce Hornsby's piano style.

The same voicings are then repeated in measures 5–8, now with the left hand adding a root note on beat 4 to increase the energy a little. Then beginning in measure 9, the right-hand triads are arpeggiated between the main rhythmic accents, using a mix of eighth- and 16th-note figures. In measure 13, the right hand adds 16th-note arpeggios inside beat 4, and the left hand adds an octave figure that anticipates beat 4 by a 16th note. These successive embellishments help to build the momentum of the groove. All of these rhythms and voicings are signature Bruce Hornsby devices.

The next comping example is in the style of "The Valley Road," which shows Bruce Hornsby's more up-tempo rock 'n' roll side:

Comping example #8 – Style of "The Valley Road" by Bruce Hornsby

TRACK 70
piano only

TRACK 71
piano plus
rhythm section

On Track 71, an electric guitar part has again been added to the bass and drums on the left channel.

You'll notice that this example alternates between measures in 4/4 time (with four beats) and measures in 2/4 time (with two beats). Adding one or more 2/4 measures to a song that is predominantly in 4/4 is a technique used in some contemporary jazz and more sophisticated pop and rock songs. Here the left-hand pattern (root-5th, root-6th on each chord) has been borrowed from blues and blues-rock styles.

In measures 1–8 the right hand plays whole note triads in the 4/4 measures, and a rhythmic upbeat (halfway through beat 2) in the 2/4 measures. Then in measures 9-16 the right-hand triad figure gets busier (landing on beat 1, halfway through beat 2, and on beat 4) in the 4/4 measures. As with the previous blues-rock examples, make sure that the left-hand pattern is steady and even, in order to give strong support to the right-hand triads!

Our final Bruce Hornsby-influenced comping example is in the style of his famous rock ballad "Mandolin Rain":

Comping example #9 – Style of "Mandolin Rain" by Bruce Hornsby

TRACK 72
piano only

TRACK 73
piano plus
rhythm section

On Track 73, a synthesizer string (chordal) part has been added to the bass and drums on the left channel.

This simple ballad example starts out in measures 1–4 with voicings and rhythms similar to example #7 (Tracks 68/69), but at a slower tempo. Again, note the triad-over-root and suspended voicings used. Then beginning in measure 5, the left hand adds a root note halfway through beat 3, leading into the 16th-note triad arpeggio that starts on beat 4 in the right hand.

Ben Folds

Ben Folds burst onto the scene in the mid-1990s with a powerful yet thoughtful rock keyboard style, both as a solo artist and with his band the Ben Folds Five (which was actually a trio). His highly rhythmic style may owe something to the fact that he is also an accomplished bassist and drummer! Our first Ben Folds-influenced comping example is in the style of his classic mid-tempo rocker "Brick":

Comping example #10 — Style of "Brick" by Ben Folds

TRACK 74
piano only

TRACK 75
piano plus
rhythm section

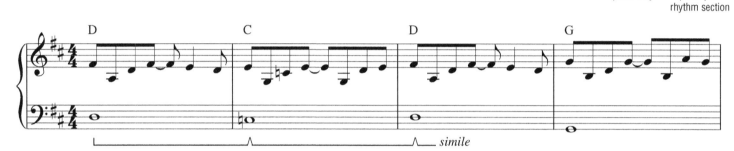

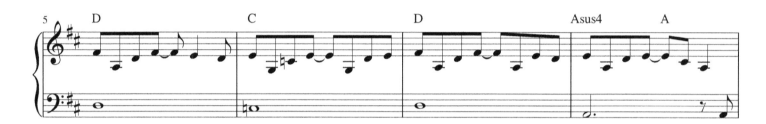

There are two very useful rock keyboard styles demonstrated in this example. In measures 1–8, the right hand is playing an eighth-note arpeggio pattern based on the chord changes, and anticipating beat 3—very typical for this style. The left hand is supporting this with a simple whole-note root pattern.

Then beginning in measure 9, we pick up the energy by adding a steady eighth-note pulse in the left-hand part, now accompanied with triad voicings in the right hand. The extra upbeats in the right hand (halfway through beat 3, in measures 9, 11, and 13–14) add forward motion to the groove. Note the use of triad-over-root chords in measures 9 and 12-13. (The B minor triad is built from the 3rd of the Gmaj7 chord, and the D major triad is built from the 3rd of the Bm7 chord.)

The next comping example is in the style of "Song for the Dumped," and shows Ben Folds's more driving blues-rock side:

Comping example #11 – Style of "Song for the Dumped" by Ben Folds

TRACK 76
piano only

TRACK 77
piano plus
rhythm section

Although this example uses mostly a driving eighth-note rhythmic feel, note the 16ths in measures 1–2 and 5–6 (specifically, on the last 16th note of beat 1, anticipating beat 2). Used sparingly, these 16ths add a funky element to this groove. The triad voicings in these measures have doubled octaves. For example the top note of the first triad (C) is also doubled one octave lower, adding more weight and power to these chords. Note also the D♯ grace notes in the right-hand part, which lead into the 3rd (E) of the C major chords. The steady eighth notes in the left hand also add to the forward motion of the example.

In measures 3–4 and 7–8 we are also using IV–I alternating triads (B♭ to F) over F in the bass. Then in measures 9–10 we have a different "chord rhythm," with the F and E♭ major chords landing halfway through beat 2 (and anticipating beat 3) during these measures. The arpeggios during the preceding B♭ and A♭ chords in these measures effectively lead into the chordal anticipations.

Another little theory note... We've also introduced a new chord in measure 11: the G7sus4. Back in Chapter 3, you remember that we derived all of the four-part chords in the key of C major, including the G7 (G dominant 7th) chord. Well, if we replace the 3rd of the G7 chord (B) with the 4th (C), we get the G7sus4 chord in measure 11.

Finally, notice that we're using the C Mixolydian mode during the C7 chord in measure 12. We start out with the "Mixolydian 3rd" interval of G-B♭ in the right hand, and then (keeping the top note or "drone" of B♭) the bottom note descends from G, to F, then finally to E (again approached with the grace note D♯). This all gives a nice blues-rock twist to the end of this example!

Our final Ben Folds-influenced comping example is in the style of his famous up-tempo rock song "Army." This actually has a swing-eighth subdivision, even though most of the action is on the quarter notes:

Comping example #12 – Style of "Army" by Ben Folds

TRACK 78
piano only

TRACK 79
piano plus
rhythm section

On Track 79, an electric guitar part has been added to the bass and drums on the left channel.

This example has a very strong quarter-note pulse in the right-hand part, using a mix of triads, suspensions, and four-part chords. In the first eight measures, we are playing only whole note roots in the right hand, so the swing-eighths subdivision is left to the rhythm section.

Beginning in measure 9, the left hand introduces an eighth-note pickup into beat 1 of the even-numbered measures. Make sure this lands on the swing-eighths subdivision (i.e., two-thirds of the way through beat 4), as this is the only time this pattern plays on an upbeat, apart from the last A major chord. Have fun!

Chapter 5

INTRO TO ROCK KEYBOARD SOLOING

The C and F Pentatonic Scales and Sub-Groups

You may remember that back in Chapter 3 we created the C Pentatonic scale by taking the C major scale and removing the 4th and 7th degrees:

This scale is very useful in rock keyboard soloing, due to its melodic interval structure, a combination of whole-step and minor 3rd intervals. The scale can be manipulated in various ways, including being split into groups of four notes, which I call "sub-groups," as follows:

TRACK 80
piano only

These four-note sub-groups start on successive scale degrees of the pentatonic scale, and then include four consecutive notes within the scale. For example, the first sub-group starts on C, and includes the notes C-D-E-G, consecutive notes in the scale starting from C. Then the next sub-group starts on D, and includes the notes D-E-G-A, consecutive notes in the scale starting from D, and so on. Pentatonic subgroups can contain different numbers of notes. For example, three-note groups are also common, as in C-D-E, D-E-G, E-G-A and so on), and can also descend as well as ascend.

Next we'll derive the F pentatonic scale by taking the F major scale and removing the 4th and 7th degrees:

We can also create four note sub-groups within the F pentatonic scale:

TRACK 81
piano only

Now let's use these scales and sub-groups in a simple solo example!

Soloing with Pentatonic Scales

In basic rock and country styles, we can build a pentatonic scale from the root of a major chord when soloing. In other words, we can use a C pentatonic scale over a C major chord, and an F pentatonic scale over an F major chord:

Solo example #1 – C and F Pentatonic Sub-Groups

TRACK 82
piano only

TRACK 83
piano plus
rhythm section

This solo is based on the previous pentatonic sub-groups (both ascending and descending), with some variations. Note the rhythmic phrasing of the solo that anticipates beat 3 by an eighth note, matching up with the left-hand root-5th pattern. This is common in eighth-note rock styles.

This is also an example of changing scales on a chord-by-chord basis when soloing, sometimes referred to as "playing through the changes." For example, we are using the C pentatonic scale over the C major chord in measure 1, then switching to the F pentatonic scale over the F major chord in measure 2, and so on. Of course, these scales have several notes in common, but using the notes that are found only in one scale and not both (i.e., E in the C pentatonic scale and F in the F pentatonic scale) gives the solo line shape and structure across the chord progression.

The A Minor Pentatonic Scale

Back in Chapter 3 we created the A minor pentatonic scale by taking the C pentatonic scale and re-positioning it to start on A, the **relative minor** of C:

Similar to the above use of the C pentatonic scale over the C major chord, this A minor pentatonic scale can also be used over an A minor or A minor 7th chord when building a solo. Since this scale contains the same notes as C pentatonic, the same sub-groups we used for the C pentatonic scale will work for the A minor pentatonic scale. Let's use this scale in a solo example.

Soloing with the Minor Pentatonic Scale

In rock and R&B styles, we can build a minor pentatonic scale from the root of a minor (or minor 7th) chord when soloing. In other words, we can use an A minor pentatonic scale over an A minor chord:

Solo example #2 – A Minor Pentatonic Scale Pattern

TRACK 84
piano only

TRACK 85
piano plus
rhythm section

On Track 85, an electric guitar part has been added to the bass and drums on the left channel.

This four-measure solo uses two two-measure rhythmic phrases, and the melodic contour (shape) of the second phrase is the same as the first. Another way to look at this is that (starting on the note A in measure 1) we descended through five steps in the A minor pentatonic scale (A-G-E-D-C-A), then skipped up three steps (A up to E, missing out C and D), then descended through three steps (E-D-C-A) to land on A. Then in the second two-meaure phrase we did exactly the same (i.e., descend through five steps, skip up three steps, descend through three steps) within the A minor pentatonic scale, this time starting on the note E instead of A. Sequencing your improv ideas this way—i.e., repeating similar melodic contours, but starting at different points in the scale and then staying within the scale—is a very important soloing technique.

The A and C Blues Scales

Back in Chapter 3 we created the A blues scale by adding a half-step connector between the notes D and E within the A minor pentatonic scale:

If we re-create the same interval pattern starting on the note C, we get a C blues scale:

Whereas the previous pentatonic scales are commonly used when "playing through the changes" (changing scales on a chord-by-chord basis), the unique melodic character of the blues scale often enables it to be used over the whole song, or a section of a song. (This is sometimes called playing "over the changes.") This soloing approach is particularly suitable for blues and blues-rock styles, as we are about to see!

Soloing with the Blues Scale

Back in Chapter 3 (Tracks 50/51) we were introduced to the 12-bar blues progression in C. Now we'll see how to construct a solo over this progression, using the C blues scale:

Solo example #3 – C Blues Scale over 12-bar Blues in C

TRACK 86
piano only

TRACK 87
piano plus
rhythm section

Note that the right-hand solo consists of a four-measure phrase that is repeated three times in total. You'll hear that the repetition of this phrase over the different chords sometimes creates vertical dissonances between the scale tones and the chord. Generally, however, the ear forgives these contradictions, due to the unique melodic strength of the blues scale. Use this example as a starting point for your own blues improvisation! The left hand is supporting the right-hand solo phrases with a basic root-5th, root-6th pattern played as quarter notes.

Adding Drone Notes Above the Blues Scale

To kick your blues scale solos or fills up a notch, try adding "drone notes" above your solo phrases. A drone note is a repeated or held note, normally played with the pinky of the right hand, added to the solo phrases that are played with the other fingers of the right hand. Favorite choices for drone notes in the blues scale are the tonic and flatted 7th degrees (C and B♭, respectively, within the C blues scale). Our final solo example now adds drone notes from the C blues scale, to the previous solo in Tracks 86/87:

Solo example #4 – C Blues Scale with Drone Notes, over 12-bar Blues in C

TRACK 88
piano only

TRACK 89
piano plus
rhythm section

On Track 89, an electric guitar part has been added to the bass and drums on the left channel.

Comparing this example to the previous solo in Tracks 86/87, note that the drone note of C (the tonic, or first degree, of the C blues scale) has been added above the solo phrase in measures 1, 5, and 9. Also, the drone note of B♭ (the ♭7th degree of the C blues scale) has been added above the solo phrase in measures 2, 6, and 10.

Meanwhile, the left hand has switched to the busier eighth-note root-5th, root-6th pattern that we first saw back in Chapter 3, which gives good rhythmic and harmonic support to the right-hand solo phrases. Good luck with your rock keyboard soloing!

Chapter 6

STYLE FILE

I n this chapter we have five tunes written in different rock keyboard styles: **pop/rock, alternative rock, classic rock, hard rock,** and **blues/rock**. The keyboard parts for these tunes focus mainly on comping—chordal accompaniments normally played by the rock keyboardist. These examples use mostly a mix of triads (with some suspensions) and arpeggios in the right hand, and either single-note, octave, root-5th, or chordal patterns in the left hand. In tunes #2 and #5, the keyboard also plays an improvised solo in the right hand, over a chord progression from an earlier section of the tune.

The main keyboard part for these tunes was recorded using an acoustic piano sound, except for tune #1 where an electric piano sound was used. In addition to the bass and drums, other instruments have been added to flesh out the arrangements: organ, acoustic and electric guitar, synthesizers, and so on. Sometimes the synth is playing the melody, which is then accompanied by the keyboard part, and sometimes the synth is playing a sustained chordal part called a "pad."

As we work through each tune, it's helpful if we can label the different sections—for example, A section or Verse, B section or Chorus, C Section or Bridge, Solo, Coda, etc. In this chapter we will use the labels "A," "B," and "C" (also known as "rehearsal letters") as we are focusing on the instrumental parts. However, as rock music is a vocal-oriented style, be aware that labels such as "Verse," "Chorus," and "Bridge" are also commonly used. These examples also all have a separate Coda section, which is the end part of the tune.

On the audio tracks, the band (minus the keyboard) are on the left channel, and the keyboard is on the right channel. To play along with the band on these tunes, just turn down the right channel. Slow, as well as Full Speed, tracks are also provided for each song.

1. Turn Out the Light

Our first tune is a pop/rock example in the style of "Kiss on My List" by Hall and Oates, with Daryl Hall on keyboards. This is a straight-eighths groove in the key of D minor, recorded with an electric piano sound. The A section begins with a series of suspended triads (sus2 and sus4 voicings), similar to Tracks 46/47 in Chapter 3. Here the steady eighth-note rhythmic comping in the right hand, is typical of mid-1980s pop/rock. Halfway through the A section in measure 9, electric guitar arpeggios are added on the left channel.

The rhythmic feel changes during the B section, with the right hand playing inverted triads (full and partial) on beats 1, halfway though beat 2, and beat 4 of each measure. This is accompanied by an arpeggiated left-hand part during beats 1 and 2, playing either root-5th-root patterns, or open triads with an overall span of greater than an octave. An organ part doubles the right-hand piano melody in this section, and a synth melody is added halfway through, in measure 25.

The organ and guitar then continue into the C section, with the piano resuming the eighth-note triad pattern used earlier, now switching between the keys of D major and F major. The synth melody is added halfway through this section (in measure 41), continuing into the Coda section in measures 49–57.

Make sure you play the right-hand eighth-note triads (in the A, C and Coda sections) crisply and evenly. The contrasting feel in the B section requires a smooth, legato playing style. Use the sustain pedal here as indicated.

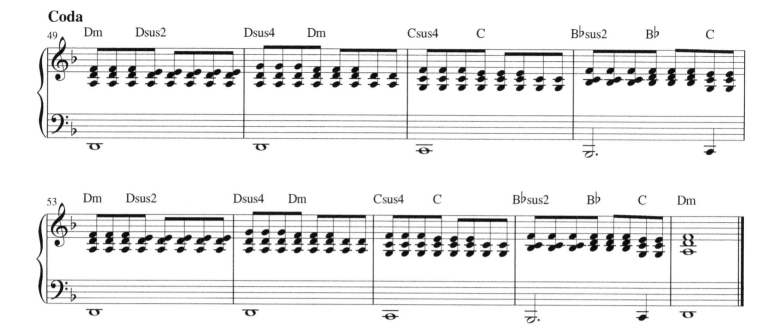

2. Shooting Star

Next up is an alternative rock example in the style of "Drops of Jupiter" by Train, with Brandon Bush on piano). This is a 16th-note groove in the key of C major, recorded with an acoustic piano sound. In the first A section (labeled "A1"), the piano part begins with triad voicings, utilizing suspensions and alternating triads. In the odd-numbered measures the right hand is playing an important rhythmic figure, landing on beat 1, halfway through beat 3, and on the second 16th-note inside beat 4. Together with landing on beat 1 of the following measure, this creates a typical 16th-note rock (as well as R&B/funk) rhythmic groove. Halfway through this section, in measure 5, an atmospheric synth pad joins in to fill out the sound.

This right-hand piano pattern continues into the first B section (adding 16th-note fills to lead into beat 3 of each measure), supported by the left hand playing the root and 5th of each chord on beats 1 and 2. The piano solo section then occurs during measures 17–32, repeating the chord changes from the A and B sections of the tune, and accompanied by an electric guitar comping part. The piano solo is mostly targeting the chord tones of the progression (i.e., landing on the 5th of the C and B♭ chords in measures 17–18, landing on the 3rd of the F chord in measure 19, and so on), and staying within a C Mixolydian mode that is the harmonic basis of this chord progression. During the last section of the solo (measures 29–32), the right hand switches to a chordal part, to build the energy further at this point.

The second A section (beginning in measure 33) is based on the first, adding 16th-note fills from pentatonic scales. Then in the second B section, the piano plays a melody part in octaves with the right hand, supported by triad voicings in the left hand. Finally in the Coda (measures 49–52), the right hand plays a mix of triads and suspensions, mostly over left-hand root-5th voicings.

Make sure that you play the right-hand 16th-note figures (i.e., on the second 16th-note of beat 4) cleanly and accurately, which is important for this type of alternative rock groove. When playing the solo section, ensure that the right-hand part projects over the left-hand voicings, and of course feel free to improvise your own solo ideas over these chord changes!

A1

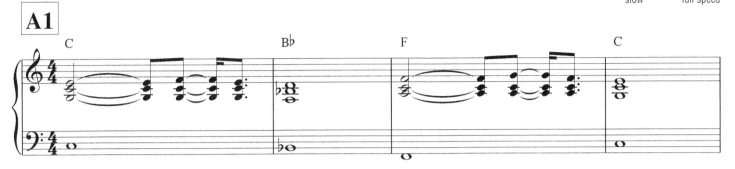

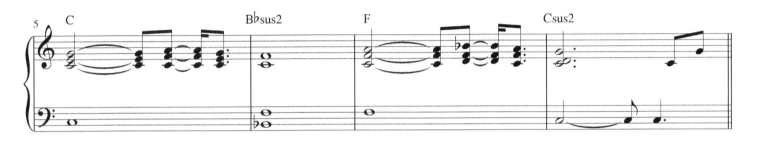

B1

(pedal simile until solo)

Solo

3. Thinking About Tomorrow

Our next example is in the classic rock style of "Don't Stop" by Fleetwood Mac. This is a swing-eighths (shuffle) groove in the key of E major, recorded with an acoustic piano sound. In the first A section we are using a bass pedal tone (similar to Tracks 64/65 in Chapter 4), alternating different triads in the right hand over a repeated bass note of E in the left hand. Note the important rhythmic characteristics of this piano groove: the right-hand triads are landing on beat 1 and halfway through beat 2 (anticipating beat 3), and the left hand plays all the eighth-note subdivisions with an alternating octave pattern. An acoustic guitar strumming pattern is also present from the beginning, complementing the piano rhythms—again, typical for this style.

In the C section the piano is playing 3rd intervals from a B Mixolydian mode, over the B7 chord (see Tracks 48/49 in Chapter 3), doubled by an electric organ part. Here the left hand takes a break from the previous octave pattern, mostly playing whole notes. The second A and B sections are a repeat of the first, now with the organ doubling the right-hand triads in the piano part. Finally the Coda section is based on the B section of the tune, with an extra four-measure tag (added section) for the final ending.

The basis of this whole groove is the swing-eighths octave pattern in the left hand, so make sure that this is solid and "in the pocket." Also ensure that the right-hand triad rhythms "lock up" with the left-hand pattern, particularly when anticipating beat 3.

TRACK 94
slow

TRACK 95
full speed

4. On My Way

Next up is a hard rock ballad in the style of "Home Sweet Home" by Motley Crue. This is a 16th-note groove in the key of F major, recorded with an acoustic piano sound. The first A section begins with piano only, with right-hand triads in an alternating-eighth ballad style. This is embellished with 16th-note arpeggios during beat 4 of each measure.

In the first B section the bass and drums enter on the left channel, and the piano part switches to a steady quarter-note pulse in the right hand, playing a mix of triads and suspensions. Note the left-hand octave pattern here that lands halfway through beats 2 and 4, in between the right-hand triads. The second A section is based on the first, now with the right hand thumb doubling the top note one octave lower, resulting in three triad tones on each downbeat (instead of two) for a more powerful sound. The left hand also switches to a half-note pattern, and an electric organ part is added at this point to further fill out the sound.

The same right-hand pattern continues into the second B section, now joined by a heavy, distorted electric guitar part to raise the energy level. The C Section is based on the chord progression from the B section, now with a different piano melody part: a mix of triads and filled-in octaves (an octave with another note in between). This piano melody is then doubled with a string synth part in this section. Finally, the Coda section is based on the progression used in the A Section, now with a low single-note guitar part doubling the bass line, a staple arranging technique in hard rock styles.

You should aim for good dynamic contrasts when playing this piece, which builds from the delicate feel of the first A section up to the high-energy feel of the second B section, and then down through to the Coda section. Also, make sure that the melody projects well in the C section, and that the 16th-note pickups are articulated cleanly in the right hand.

A2

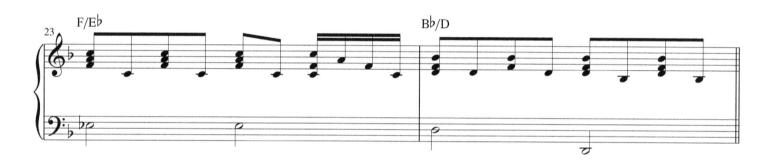

B2

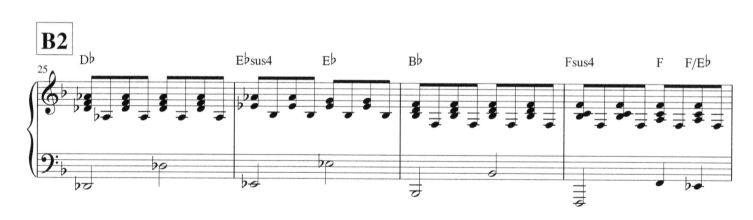

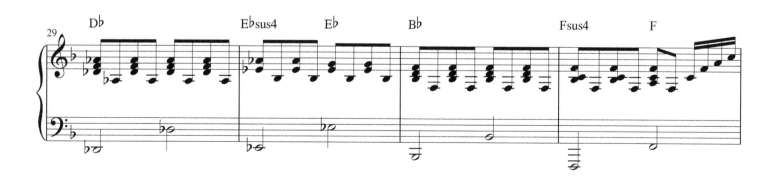

C

Coda

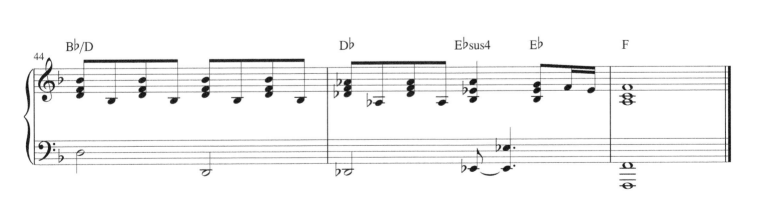

5. Working Overtime

Our final example in this chapter is in the blues-rock style of "Takin' Care of Business" by Bachman-Turner Overdrive, with Norman Durkee on piano. This is a straight-eighths groove in the key of A major, recorded with an acoustic piano sound. Throughout this piece, the left hand is playing a driving root-5th, root-6th interval pattern, a staple of blues-rock piano styles. The first A section starts with a simple triad rhythm in the right hand, landing on beat 1 and halfway through beat 3 of each measure. Then beginning in measure 9, the right hand switches to a IV–I alternating triad pattern on each chord, building the intensity in this section.

In the B section, the right hand switches to playing Mixolydian 3rd interval patterns over the various dominant seventh chords (see Tracks 48/49 in Chapter 3). This is varied by playing some "♭3 to 3" movements on the dominant chords (i.e., moving from G to G♯ on the E7 chord). Then beginning in the second A section, the right hand plays the root and 5th of each chord (with the top note doubled one octave below) on all the eighth-note subdivisions, varied with a "♭5 to 5" movement (i.e., moving from D♯ to E on the A chord) in measures 37–40. All this is typical of blues-rock piano styles.

In the Solo section (measures 41–48), the right hand is using two-measure phrases from the A blues scale, with drone notes added during the last four measures (see Tracks 86–89 in Chapter 5). Finally in the Coda section, the "♭5 to 5" movement is reintroduced over the F, G, and A chords (with the root on top as the drone note), and the A blues scale (with the drone note of G on top) is used in measure 52 on the D7 chord, and for the unison riff in measure 56.

As with most piano blues styles, make sure the left hand pattern is rock solid across the different chord changes. You will benefit from practicing this part separately before adding the right hand. In the solo section, ensure that the right-hand part projects over the left-hand pattern, and of course feel free to experiment with your own blues piano solo ideas!

TRACK 98
slow

TRACK 99
full speed

APPENDIX

Major Scales

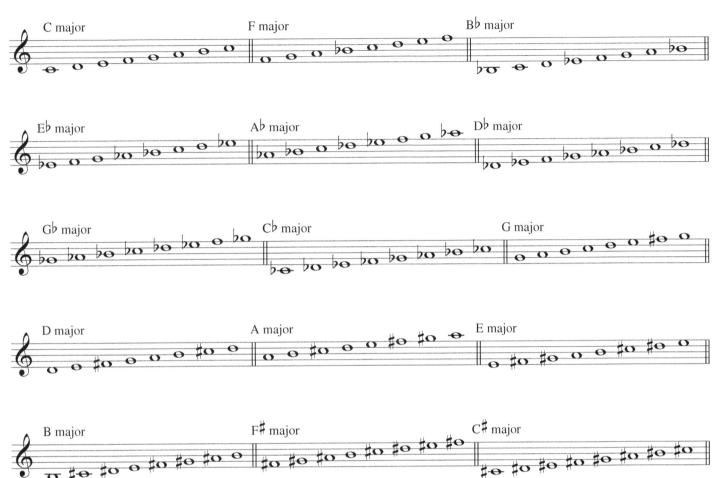

Key Signatures

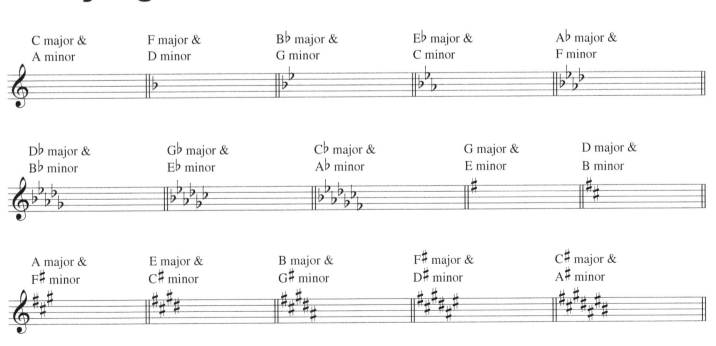

Mixolydian Modes

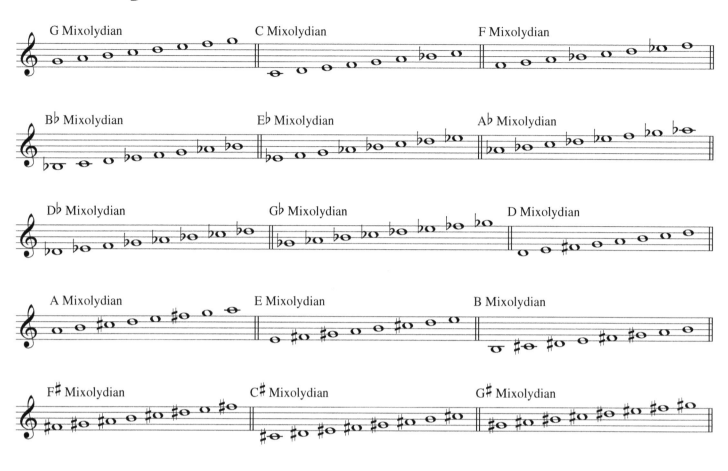

Pentatonic scales

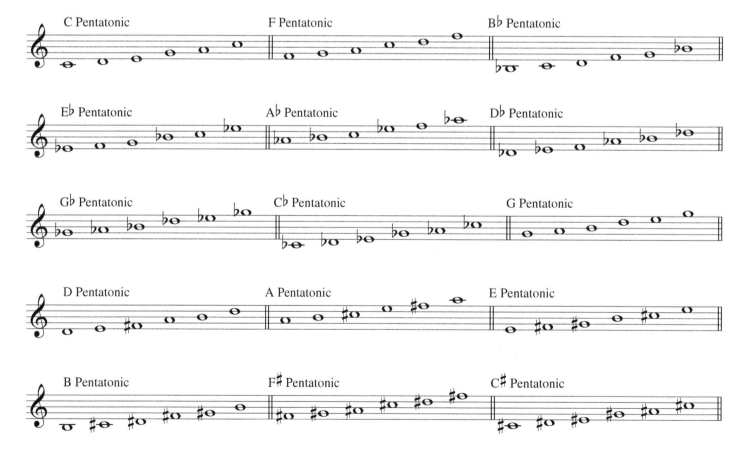

Minor Pentatonic scales

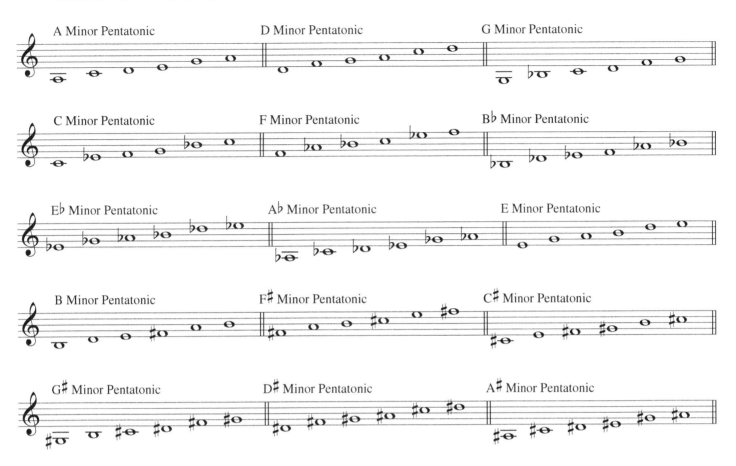

Blues scales

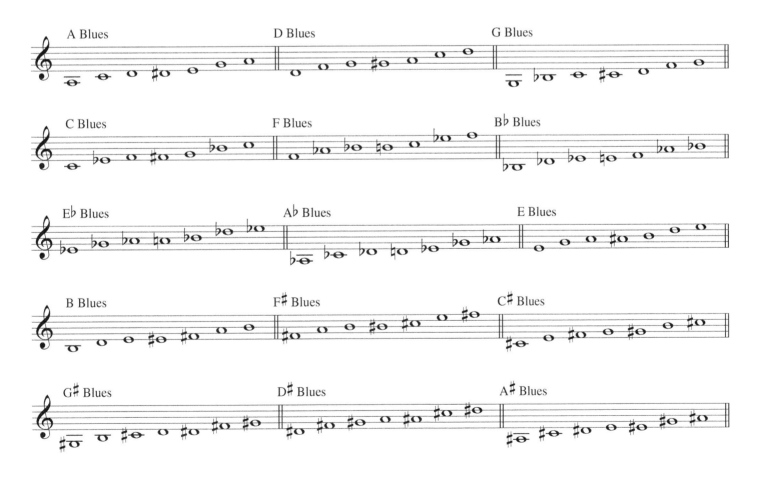

KEYBOARD STYLE SERIES

THE COMPLETE GUIDE!

These book/audio packs provide focused lessons that contain valuable how-to insight, essential playing tips, and beneficial information for all players. From comping to soloing, comprehensive treatment is given to each subject. The companion audio features many of the examples in the book performed either solo or with a full band.

BEBOP JAZZ PIANO
by John Valerio
This book provides detailed information for bebop and jazz keyboardists on: chords and voicings, harmony and chord progressions, scales and tonality, common melodic figures and patterns, comping, characteristic tunes, the styles of Bud Powell and Thelonious Monk, and more.
00290535 Book/Online Audio $18.99

BEGINNING ROCK KEYBOARD
by Mark Harrison
This comprehensive book/audio package will teach you the basic skills needed to play beginning rock keyboard. From comping to soloing, you'll learn the theory, the tools, and the techniques used by the pros. The accompanying audio demonstrates most of the music examples in the book.
00311922 Book/Online Audio $14.99

BLUES PIANO
by Mark Harrison
With this book/audio pack, you'll learn the theory, the tools, and even the tricks that the pros use to play the blues. Covers: scales and chords; left-hand patterns; walking bass; endings and turnarounds; right-hand techniques; how to solo with blues scales; crossover licks; and more.
00311007 Book/Online Audio $19.99

BOOGIE-WOOGIE PIANO
by Todd Lowry
From learning the basic chord progressions to inventing your own melodic riffs, you'll learn the theory, tools and techniques used by the genre's best practicioners.
00117067 Book/Online Audio $17.99

BRAZILIAN PIANO
by Robert Willey and Alfredo Cardim
Brazilian Piano teaches elements of some of the most appealing Brazilian musical styles: choro, samba, and bossa nova. It starts with rhythmic training to develop the fundamental groove of Brazilian music.
00311469 Book/Online Audio $19.99

CONTEMPORARY JAZZ PIANO
by Mark Harrison
From comping to soloing, you'll learn the theory, the tools, and the techniques used by the pros. The full band tracks on the audio feature the rhythm section on the left channel and the piano on the right channel, so that you can play along with the band.
00311848 Book/Online Audio $18.99

COUNTRY PIANO
by Mark Harrison
Learn the theory, the tools, and the tricks used by the pros to get that authentic country sound. This book/audio pack covers: scales and chords, walkup and walkdown patterns, comping in traditional and modern country, Nashville "fretted piano" techniques and more.
00311052 Book/Online Audio $19.99

GOSPEL PIANO
by Kurt Cowling
Discover the tools you need to play in a variety of authentic gospel styles, through a study of rhythmic devices, grooves, melodic and harmonic techniques, and formal design. The accompanying audio features over 90 tracks, including piano examples as well as the full gospel band.
00311327 Book/Online Adio $17.99

INTRO TO JAZZ PIANO
by Mark Harrison
From comping to soloing, you'll learn the theory, the tools, and the techniques used by the pros. The accompanying audio demonstrates most of the music examples in the book. The full band tracks feature the rhythm section on the left channel and the piano on the right channel, so that you can play along with the band.
00312088 Book/Online Audio $17.99

JAZZ-BLUES PIANO
by Mark Harrison
This comprehensive book will teach you the basic skills needed to play jazz-blues piano. Topics covered include: scales and chords • harmony and voicings • progressions and comping • melodies and soloing • characteristic stylings.
00311243 Book/Online Audio $17.99

JAZZ-ROCK KEYBOARD
by T. Lavitz
Learn what goes into mixing the power and drive of rock music with the artistic elements of jazz improvisation in this comprehensive book and CD package. This instructional tool delves into scales and modes, and how they can be used with various chord progressions to develop the best in soloing chops.
00290536 Book/CD Pack..........................$17.95

LATIN JAZZ PIANO
by John Valerio
This book is divided into three sections. The first covers Afro-Cuban (Afro-Caribbean) jazz, the second section deals with Brazilian influenced jazz – Bossa Nova and Samba, and the third contains lead sheets of the tunes and instructions for the play-along audio.
00311345 Book/Online Audio $17.99

MODERN POP KEYBOARD
by Mark Harrison
From chordal comping to arpeggios and ostinatos, from grand piano to synth pads, you'll learn the theory, the tools, and the techniques used by the pros. The online audio demonstrates most of the music examples in the book.
00146596 Book/Online Audio $17.99

NEW AGE PIANO
by Todd Lowry
From melodic development to chord progressions to left-hand accompaniment patterns, you'll learn the theory, the tools and the techniques used by the pros. The accompanying 96-track CD demonstrates most of the music examples in the book.
00117322 Book/CD Pack..........................$16.99

POST-BOP JAZZ PIANO
by John Valerio
This book/audio pack will teach you the basic skills needed to play post-bop jazz piano. Learn the theory, the tools, and the tricks used by the pros to play in the style of Bill Evans, Thelonious Monk, Herbie Hancock, McCoy Tyner, Chick Corea and others. Topics covered include: chord voicings, scales and tonality, modality, and more.
00311005 Book/Online Audio $17.99

PROGRESSIVE ROCK KEYBOARD
by Dan Maske
You'll learn how soloing techniques, form, rhythmic and metrical devices, harmony, and counterpoint all come together to make this style of rock the unique and exciting genre it is.
00311307 Book/Online Audio $19.99

R&B KEYBOARD
by Mark Harrison
From soul to funk to disco to pop, you'll learn the theory, the tools, and the tricks used by the pros with this book/audio pack. Topics covered include: scales and chords, harmony and voicings, progressions and comping, rhythmic concepts, characteristic stylings, the development of R&B, and more! Includes seven songs.
00310881 Book/Online Audio $19.99

ROCK KEYBOARD
by Scott Miller
Learn to comp or solo in any of your favorite rock styles. Listen to the audio to hear your parts fit in with the total groove of the band. Includes 99 tracks! Covers: classic rock, pop/rock, blues rock, Southern rock, hard rock, progressive rock, alternative rock and heavy metal.
00310823 Book/Online Audio $17.99

ROCK 'N' ROLL PIANO
by Andy Vinter
Take your place alongside Fats Domino, Jerry Lee Lewis, Little Richard, and other legendary players of the '50s and '60s! This book/audio pack covers: left-hand patterns; basic rock 'n' roll progressions; right-hand techniques; straight eighths vs. swing eighths; glisses, crushed notes, rolls, note clusters and more. Includes six complete tunes.
00310912 Book/Online Audio $18.99

SALSA PIANO
by Hector Martignon
From traditional Cuban music to the more modern Puerto Rican and New York styles, you'll learn the all-important rhythmic patterns of salsa and how to apply them to the piano. The book provides historical, geographical and cultural background info, and the 50+-tracks includes piano examples and a full salsa band percussion section.
00311049 Book/Online Audio $19.99

SMOOTH JAZZ PIANO
by Mark Harrison
Learn the skills you need to play smooth jazz piano – the theory, the tools, and the tricks used by the pros. Topics covered include: scales and chords; harmony and voicings; progressions and comping; rhythmic concepts; melodies and soloing; characteristic stylings; discussions on jazz evolution.
00311095 Book/Online Audio $19.99

STRIDE & SWING PIANO
by John Valerio
Learn the styles of the stride and swing piano masters, such as Scott Joplin, Jimmy Yancey, Pete Johnson, Jelly Roll Morton, James P. Johnson, Fats Waller, Teddy Wilson, and Art Tatum. This book/audio pack covers classic ragtime, early blues and boogie woogie, New Orleans jazz and more. Includes 14 songs.
00310882 Book/Online Audio $19.99

WORSHIP PIANO
by Bob Kauflin
From chord inversions to color tones, from rhythmic patterns to the Nashville Numbering System, you'll learn the tools and techniques needed to play piano or keyboard in a modern worship setting.
00311425 Book/Online Audio $17.99

HAL•LEONARD®

Prices, contents, and availability
subject to change without notice.

www.halleonard.com